GET ELECTED,

Make A Difference!

GET ELECTED,
Make A Difference!

A "how-to" book
for the person interested in seeking
public office at the City, County or State level.
Written by a person who has done it
successfully.

▼

By:
State Representative Rich Becker
*A community activist, he has served as a city councilman
and four terms as mayor of Lenexa, Kansas, one of the
nation's fastest-growing cities. He is now a representative in
the Kansas Legislature. He learned how to "Get Elected."*

GET ELECTED, MAKE A DIFFERENCE!: A "how-to" book for the person interested in seeking public office at the local, city, county, or state level. Written by a person who has done it successfully.

Copyright © 1996 by Rich Becker

All rights reserved, including the right to reproduce this book or portions thereof in any form.

Edited by: Leathers Publishing, Prairie Village, KS

Published and printed in the United States of America.

ISBN: 0-9648941-0-6

Library of Congress Catalog Card Number: 95-92574

Publication date: January 1996

Published and Distributed by:
Pump-Em-Up Publishing
PO Box 14934
9225 Woodstone Lane
Shawnee Mission, KS 66285
Phone/Fax 913-894-9530

Dedication

▼
―――――――――――――――――――――――――

To my wife Nancy.
Thanks for everything.

You can do anything you're big enough to do if you have a big enough heart and a big enough spirit.

—State Representative Rich Becker

Introduction

I've been interested in public service for a long time. As a kid growing up in St. Louis, I saw my parents do what they considered their duty to be a part of the system. My father was the Justice of Peace and committeeman, and Mother was the committee woman in the area where we lived in south St. Louis. Back in those days, they knew almost everybody who lived within a six- or seven-square-block area. That meant if a family needed food, or somebody needed a job, or somebody had a problem with a city service, etc., they would contact my parents, who would contact somebody else "up the line," and the person in need was taken care of. It was no problem for Dad and Mom. That was the way the system worked. They both believed in the process, as I do, and no doubt you do, too. Yet it's a different world today. People move around perhaps too often, and what worked then just doesn't always work now. Our neighbors aren't always our friends. In many places people don't know, or even care to know, the people next door or down the street.

It was after I grew up in St. Louis, served in the Navy, moved to Kansas City, got married and started a family that it became very clear what my dad used to say was true.

"As you grow up, you will find things that you are not happy with. You can change things! You *can* fight city hall! You can have a say in the government that controls your life, but *you must get involved.*" Over the years, I have found that his advice was absolutely correct.

My first experience was when I was very unhappy with some aspects of our school system. The neighborhood we moved to had hundreds of elementary school-age children and many more on the way. Yet the policy of the school board at that time was to bus these children to distant schools that were not crowded. They did this in lieu of building a new school. So I went into action. Along with a good friend, we made a presentation to the school board, asking for a new school in our area. That launched our attack. We became very active. We gathered the troops, had aerial photos made, distributed literature, had many informational meetings, etc. For a year and a half I attended every school board meeting (which was one of the most excruciating experiences of my life). But we won. We did get a school for our kids, followed over the years by several more in our community. It all started by being involved, being an activist, and wanting to get something done, and doing something about it.

That experience got me active. From then on, some people considered me to be the local "activist," "hell-raiser" or whatever. Some people would actually go out of their way to avoid meeting me, because they were sick and tired of hearing about the "school issue." Negative and positive, I made a name for myself. From some, I was called very uncomplimentary names. But I had a mission and, in my mind, I was right. I was one of the few who was willing to stand up for what I believed in, and fight to get schools for our kids. From that and other experiences, I have learned a great deal about people through my involvement in many different issues.

This book is written to help those of you who—like myself—have an interest in getting involved, and who want to make a difference. Unfortunately, there are some people who like to raise hell about an issue but don't want to be part of or help find a solution to a problem.

To make the biggest impact, you have to get elected to a position so you can, in fact, be in a position to change the system. Otherwise, you can yell and scream forever, but unless you are in an elected position where you can effect change in public policy, all you can do is yell and scream. Without this book, your noise will have little effect on the way things are done.

I saved many notes and papers and clippings of my years serving as a City Councilman, as a Mayor, and now as a State Representative. I have had wonderful experiences of winning campaigns, and heartbreak for a short time when I lost an election. All these experiences have contributed to my understanding of what it takes to get elected and make a difference.

Those I won, as well as the races for the School Board and Governor that I did not win and the experience of having worked on a large number of campaigns for all kinds of elected offices, taught me well. In addition, there were lessons learned while recently serving as the Chairman of a county sales tax election to build a new jail. All this gave me an understanding of how to get elected to a local and state office and make a difference.

The purpose of this book is to give you the information you need and also inspiration. I've tried to cover all the bases without getting too technical. So read on, because the next step is up to you.

The Best Advice from National Political Leaders

▼

A book on how to get elected to public office would be incomplete without the expert opinions of some of the leading political leaders in the United States. They have all been very involved in their communities and very involved in many political races.

I asked a number of them what was the best advice they ever received regarding campaigning and getting elected. What they told me is located at the beginning of each chapter. It is pretty basic solid information—and worth careful reading.

Since the person reading and using this how-to book in many cases is a person who is either now seeking or thinking about seeking a local or state public office, the comments from these leaders could be invaluable. My sincere thanks to those political leaders who took a few minutes of precious time to help the person who wants to run for public office and make a difference.

The Best Advice from
U.S. Senator Bob Dole of Kansas

>"In 1950 when I was first elected to the Kansas Legislature, a reporter asked if I had a legislative agenda.
>
>I replied, 'I'm going to sit and watch for a couple of days and then I'll stand up for what I think is right.'"

Contents

Foreword by Senator Nancy Landon Kassebaum 13

Chapter 1	First Things First	15
Chapter 2	Single Issue Candidate	23
Chapter 3	Gathering the Troops	31
Chapter 4	Getting Ready to Run	41
Chapter 5	Organization/Steering Committee	65
Chapter 6	Campaign Strategy and Tactics	79
Chapter 7	Lists/Polls/Surveys	115
Chapter 8	Budget	121
Chapter 9	Fund-raising	127
Chapter 10	Direct Mail/Mailings/Literature	141
Chapter 11	Research	149
Chapter 12	Issues	169
Chapter 13	Grass-roots Campaigning	173
Chapter 14	Get Exposure/Advertising/Publicity	199

Chapter 15	Volunteers and Campaign Workers	249
Chapter 16	Debates/Forums	253
Chapter 17	GOTV—Get Out the Vote	261
Chapter 18	Absentee Voters	265
Chapter 19	Legalities of a Campaign	267
Chapter 20	Civics 101 Vs. the Real World	269
Chapter 21	Campaign Schedule	273
Chapter 22	Wisdom, Thoughts, Truisms and Quotes	289

Foreword
By Senator Nancy Landon Kassebaum

▼

"Get Elected, Make a Difference!" is a "how-to" book that does make a difference regarding participation in the political process. That it does so in a most practical, fundamental way is because Rich Becker is one who believes that public service is an important and honorable calling.

Far too often it is easier to sit back and criticize without wanting to be involved. This is a book about the importance of being involved. The great strength of our political system is grass-roots participation. William Allen White wrote "Politics: The Citizen's Business" in 1924, making the case that citizens involved and engaged are essential for a democracy.

We have been seekers of reform since Paul Revere's ride. The extraordinary men who gathered in Philadelphia in 1787 argued back and forth about the scope of federal government and the rights of the states and individuals. The debate continues today.

Rich Becker lays out the blueprint for us to be engaged in the citizen's business. The Founding Fathers didn't have a script, computers, cellular phones and fax machines—but they did have a certain knowledge of human behavior. They were able to give depth and perspective to the issues of the time and to create a framework for self-government that has endured across two centuries.

Today the demands of special constituencies for increased governmental intervention against the resistance of the public to further growth of governmental power has become an incessant drumbeat. Yet, the basic issues of our nation remain the same, and our dedication to family, community and country remain the core values of our public life.

America remains a work in progress. Rich Becker's message is that *someone* must do the work. Democracy is not propelled by magic; it must be built each day by people who care, who give the time and thought necessary to the tasks of self-government at every level—in our schools, cities, counties, state legislatures and Congress. This is genuinely noble work, and a worthy calling for every person who claims the high title of "citizen."

Nancy Becker, Rich, Senator Nancy Kassebaum

Chapter 1

First Things First

The Best Advice from
U.S. Senator Ben Nighthorse Campbell of Colorado

"I must admit, I didn't really give much thought to what it would take to run and win when I accepted my first nomination for Colorado's 59th State Legislative District. In fact, it was kind of an instant decision to run for office. But I decided if I was going to be in it, I'd be very aggressive. My old coaches taught me well: the fight begins when the bell rings.

I was nominated unanimously, but I remember a lawyer stood up and told me, 'You don't have a chance. They won't elect a ponytail.'

Maybe this advice was the best thing for me. I think that it may be part of being a member of a minority. I'm not sure. But when you grow up with people telling you to avoid your past and ignore your ancestry because it will hurt you and when you're constantly told you don't have a chance, I suppose you get an idea that you've got to work twice as hard as other people to achieve the same goals. I've always done that."

If you're going to get involved, please get involved for the right reasons.

Men are supposedly driven by four desires—money, love, principles and power. The political life offers some of each.

There are more than 500,000 locally elected officials in this country. They range from citizens just like you who are elected to such positions as City Council members and Mayor, County Commissioners, County Treasurer, Sheriff, Assessor, Water Board, State Representative, State Senator, State Treasurer, Secretary of State, Governor, Local School Boards, Superintendent, Advisory Council, Ownership Trustees, and all kinds of special district boards and positions. The many elected offices available will differ from one community to another and from one state to another, but the fact remains that there are many opportunities to serve.

In politics you truly can make something happen. Let's face it, you wouldn't be reading this book unless you had an interest in getting involved and making a difference. That's good, because that is what this book is all about.

These days it is very difficult to get people involved for a variety of reasons. With your energy and my help, you can get more involved in the process.

I know that many people are reluctant to be on boards or run for elective office because they don't want to subject themselves to media scrutiny and have their personal lives investigated and criticized.

I want to take the mystery out of the process of running for and getting elected to a local or state office.

It is not for everyone. I have friends who have *no use* for politics. But, believe me, if you are concerned, like to get things done, enjoy talking to people, etc., then you're like me, and I believe you will find elected office the most rewarding experience of your life.

You don't need any special talent, and I don't care if you are a woman or a man or what your race is. But you do need desire, drive and interest in doing what is right and fair.

Some people say, "I'm just an ordinary person. What chance do I have to be elected?" Well, let me tell you that ordinary men and women are elected all the time. If you have an interest, you need to be smart about how you go about pursuing your goal. In this book I will cover the real nuts and bolts of politics, how to convince your fellow citizens to vote for you.

You have to be ready to lose as well as win. But with the right direction, you can minimize the chances to lose. My first attempt at public office was a run for the school board in our huge school district, and I lost big. As a friend of mine said, I got my laundry cleaned. Since then, I was elected to the City Council several times, and I ran for and was elected Mayor of Lenexa, Kansas, one of the fastest-growing communities in the Midwest, four times. Now I'm serving in the Kansas Legislature as a State Representative. I have been involved as a volunteer and advisor to others in many campaigns and, as I said before, most recently was Chairman of a county sales tax election to build a new jail. It passed handily. What you'll find in this book are tested and proven ways to win elections by a person who has won (and lost) elections.

Election battles are fought and won.

In this practical "how-to" book, I'll cover the behind-the-scenes action of a campaign. I will warn you about the pitfalls and mistakes many make. For starters, you may need a new way of thinking about yourself and your abilities. You'll need to use plenty of good ol' common sense and, as I like to say, you can do anything you're big enough to do. That is, if you have a big enough heart and big enough spirit.

Remember that the decisions political leaders make shape our daily lives and the lives of our children in the future. You can be one of the people making that difference.

The way you conduct a successful campaign—whether for the water board in your home town or for State Senator in your state—is generally the same. As one person told me a long time ago, getting people to vote for you is nothing more than adult show-and-tell. You show up and tell the people about yourself...sell yourself...and tell them what you're planning to do for your community, state or for them. And you ask them to vote for you. It is marketing. You have to market yourself. Like it or not, it isn't much different from the way a product is sold on television.

John F. Kennedy's advisor, Larry O'Brien, said, "Behind all political success is attention to detail."

There are no absolutes, nothing that says if you follow these rules you will be elected. But there are many things you can do to put the odds in your favor. And at the same time ensure that your time, energy and money are spent in their most productive fashion.

All of us who run for office have to face the fact that to many people "politics" is a dirty word. To them, most people involved in politics are rotten, self-serving, even corrupt.

So often, I find these are the same people who are not even registered to vote or, more likely, the ones who complain about things but are not interested in being part of the solution. Don't let these folks distract you.

Essentially, politics is nothing more than getting people of all kinds of various viewpoints together to find one common course of action. It is not an easy process, but people of good will, working together, can solve all kinds of problems. Believe me, in all my years in politics, I have found that 99.9 percent of the politicians in this world are good people. They are dedicated, caring, helpful, honest, compassionate and want to solve problems and improve the lives of their constituents and their communities. And want to do it in a straight-forward, honest and open manner.

They realize that when you are involved in politics, you have a wonderful opportunity to serve your fellow citizens and help make your community, as we say in my town, "a great place to live, work, raise a family and do business."

Becoming a candidate can be a scary experience. It has to be done with your eyes wide open. Many a good person has been encouraged to run by people whom he can't find once he has indeed filed. If you are going to run, it is your decision to make, and you have to be serious about it. You need to gather all the facts you can, talk about it with trusted friends and advisors, think more about it for a while and, as my mother used to say, "sleep on it for a while." Then you make the decision, and once you make it, don't look back. Don't waste your time and energy second-guessing yourself. You'll drive yourself crazy. Get on with it, with all you have.

I have always had a problem with people who are "talked into" running for office, or who are "talked into" serving on a board or commission, or being president of their organization. It has been my experience that when that happens, you just flat out don't have the dedication to do a good job.

If you are going to run, run to win. If you are not planning to give it all you have, don't waste your time, or that of your supporters. And when you get into it, it will take concentrated effort on your part. If you have a lack of interest or dedication, that in turn will decrease your enthusiasm, and that will become very apparent to those around you.

As an example, when I ran for mayor against a two-term incumbent, I campaigned door to door. I knocked on the door of every registered voter in the city (about 7,000 homes). For three months, almost every afternoon from after work until dark and from noon to dark on Saturday and Sunday, in rain, snow, sleet, regardless of the weather or temperature, I talked to voters and asked for their votes.

When the votes were counted on election night, I won by 168 votes out of the more than 8,000 that were cast. An interesting sidelight to that campaign is that I met many people going door to door who have been good friends and my biggest supporters in elections since then.

Not every campaign is a winner, unfortunately. Recently I ran for Governor of Kansas. The plan of action called for campaigning in each of the 627 towns in Kansas that have a Mayor. To do this, I campaigned in from six to 12 towns a day, six days a week, each week for three and a half months. It was the most extensive grass-roots campaign ever conducted in the state. With all that, I planned to win. But I didn't.

Win or lose, it takes enormous effort because there is more to running for office than signing a few papers, or collecting signature petitions, etc. Be prepared for long hours, plenty of speeches, asking people for money, attending meetings, talking to voters, making phone calls and more.

Make no mistake about it; your political involvement will affect your personal life, your job, and your general outlook on things. Before I ran for Mayor, I discussed the possibility with my wife. I made a commitment that if I won we would both be very involved. I did win, and during the 12 years as Mayor, she attended meetings, rallies, dinners and events. That was important to me and any candidate who is married. A supportive spouse makes a difference.

In my political life, I have known many an elected official who had a spouse who hated politics. That makes for a difficult situation—but one you have to deal with. I realized a long time ago that not everybody loves politics as I do. Or says as I do that one of the greatest satisfactions in the world is being able to actually get things done that benefit your fellow citizens.

Get Elected, Make a Difference!

Rich promoting his city where he served as Mayor for 12 years.

Chapter 2

Single Issue Candidate

▼

The Best Advice from
Congressman Gil GutKnecht of Minnesota

"Never turn your back on your base."

Some candidates get involved because they are very upset over one specific action of an elected official or a board or believe in one specific philosophy or issue. Someone got fired, or they voted against or for a specific issue such as abortion.

To get elected, a single-issue candidate must voice the strong community sentiment over this or that emotional issue. Don't let your obsession with a particular issue blur your good judgment. As my dad used to say, "Act in haste, and you can repent at leisure." To me, a person who is interested in only one issue does himself and the citizens a disservice by running for office.

And don't waste your time, energy or money trying to be a "symbolic" candidate. That is, the person who really doesn't run to win, but who runs to make a point, to protest, or to try to educate voters to his or her point of view. Issue-oriented movements very often have candidates who carry their message to the voters. These campaigns generally don't have wide community appeal. Their goal is not necessarily to win, but mainly to help spread the word about the issue and gather new supporters for the movement. If that person can get enough votes (even though he doesn't win), he will be seen as representing a constituency that the winner will have to deal with as he or she carries out the duties of the office.

After all, the electorate would have to be very dissatisfied with their present elected official to give much support to a rival who is concerned more with protesting than with winning. It is unlikely that a voter would go to the polls and vote for anybody if they felt they were throwing away their vote.

If you are going to run for an office, make sure the job you want is one that you truly feel comfortable with, and one you sincerely are interested in serving. You will notice that I did not say, "Make sure it is an office you can win," because I believe with the right circumstances and the right plan of action, almost any state or local office is winnable. And if you have a desire to run, make your intentions known loud and clear. It is amazing how many good people are available to help you in your quest. And since political winds shift pretty fast, you need to move quickly. An opportunity today might be locked up by someone else—often someone who is less qualified than you.

In making a decision to run or not, you first must do your homework. That involves, among other things, research into past voting patterns for the office you are seeking. (We'll discuss that later in this book.) You should feel out the opinions of other community leaders. They are great sounding boards for anyone considering public office. You also need to find out who your opponent's enemies are—because he or she most likely has them. We all have them. It's especially true that any incumbent who has had to vote on issues or take public stands has people out there who are not happy with the officeholder. Then get out in the field and learn what's on their minds. Talk to people all over the community or state to get a feel for how "Betty Smith on 83rd Street" feels about the issues and what is on her mind. Talk to political leaders, too. Tune into the political grapevine to get an earful about what is going on in the political world. Fill yourself with knowledge.

As you make the rounds, you will find plenty of words of encouragement and support. People appreciate someone who risks running for office. But don't let your head get too big until those words turn into real support like receiving their substantial check or personal endorsement. Or volunteer to help in other ways. Just continue to ask questions, ask for support, ask about the office, ask about other potential supporters, ask about the opposition, etc. A potential supporter may not say this to you, but the question usually in his or her mind—whether it is said or not—is "What's in it for me? Can I count on you for good government, better school system, more programs for children, a return to good ol' fashioned family values?" A business person might be concerned about taxes, a good business climate in the community, a new road so his trucks can navigate his business park better. Each supporter you pick up will have his own reason for wanting you in public office. You need to get educated. A wise person I know told me once that your real education begins after you think you know it all. Get yourself educated!

Also, you need to make an early decision to run. I can't tell you how important it is to lock up your support early. Very often good potential candidates find out that people they were counting on for support have already committed to another candidate because they did not know you were even interested. Make your interest known early.

And don't get upset when you find out that not everyone loves you. I know in my years as a public servant I have found that no matter what you do, there will be those who will not agree with you and who will oppose you. That's a given. They are the ones who feel they were born into this world to espouse the "other" viewpoint. If you want to paint the wall blue, they want to paint it red. If you say okay, in the spirit of compromise, let's paint it red, they will say let's paint it green. They usually are not interested in solving problems. They like to make a game out of raising hell.

All of this is human nature at work. When I was a kid, my parents instilled in me a love of trees and nature. I thought everybody loved trees. But when I became Mayor, I found out that there are people in this world who hate trees. Trees have leaves that have to be raked, they cast shadows so the snow won't melt, and they obstruct the view of their businesses, etc.

Now the question about your opponent:

It doesn't make a lot of sense to run against someone in your own party unless there are serious differences of opinion or unresolved philosophical differences. As you make the rounds, you'll get a good feel for what to do or not to do. Be smart, don't be an opportunist in the sense that you want to challenge a person in your same party merely for personal ambition. That could not only make you a loser, but split the party and hand the election over to the other side. And in doing it, cause you to lose valuable supporters in the future.

How about those on your team? Citizens want to be involved in the political process. Maybe not as a candidate, but as someone who has an opinion and wants to be heard. What's wrong with that? A smart candidate will gather together all these folks he can and listen to them. We all have opinions, and everyone wants to be heard.

While I was Mayor, I was always open to listening to people in person, on the phone, at events, all hours of the day and night. For 12 straight years, I would pick one day a year and invite everyone in the community to come to City Hall for "Tell the mayor what's on your mind" day.

I would sit at a table in City Hall from 8 a.m. until 10 p.m., and people would stream in and tell me about our city, one-to-one. What they liked, what they didn't like, their problems, their concerns, their complaints, etc. I found that this was the best gauge of the temperature of the city. Throughout the 14-hour day someone was sitting across from me talking about their town and their feelings. I took plenty of notes, and I forwarded the information to the respective person in the city for action. And everybody received a thank you letter for participating.

People generally hold their leaders to a higher standard than they themselves are held to. Few feel that politicians command respect. The most common reasons cited are that they have *not* demonstrated courage, or integrity, or honesty, or intelligence, or vision. Or all of the above.

So many public officials have business interests that in some fashion or other may compromise their ability to serve the public. Yet as a person who has been involved, I feel that the people sometimes are better off having someone involved in the business world representing them than someone who does not have any conflicts.

It reminds me of discussion we had at the city over a period of a year or more about an ethics ordinance. Some citizens thought it absolutely wrong for a person on the Council to discuss (much less vote on) a proposal for telephone service if the council member or anyone in his or her family owned as little as one share of stock in a phone company. I didn't agree because if you are active and involved in the community, you most likely will have conflicts. I'd rather have that person discussing and voting on things because that person generally can add intelligent thought to the issue.

As a public official, you will find that many things you do for the public good are unappreciated and unreported to the public. More about this later.

After you're elected, you will receive lots of free advice on how to do things from your friends and allies. On numerous occasions, I've had people I know come up to me and stick a traffic ticket in my coat pocket and say, "Take care of this for me, will you, Rich?" I graciously give it back to them and say with a smile that if I "fix" it, it will cost them $20 more than if they just pay it.

I had a businessman supporter send me a ticket in the mail with a note, "Will you take care of this for me?" I no doubt created an enemy out of a supporter when I sent it back to him with a note saying, "I don't fix tickets!"

Why Are You Running?

In one or two sentences you need to write down just why you are running. Why do you want to be _____? Believe me, you will be asked that question hundreds of times while campaigning. So you had better have it clear so you can repeat it verbatim over and over. Think it through carefully.

Who Asked You to Run?

I remember when I became the first candidate in the race for Governor, there was an editorial in one of the small town papers that was highly critical of me for deciding on my own that I wanted to become a candidate. When the question was asked, "Who asked you to run?" the answer was, "I did."

Don't let some newspaper editorial or some political hack tell you what you should or shouldn't do about running. Let your own good judgment guide the way after carefully talking about it to the people in your community.

Remember the one big rule of community service that must be followed if you want to then run for public office...you must work. You must perform. You must produce!

Here are a dozen things to think about:

- ❖ If you are going to be a candidate for elective office, you should be consumed with a desire to win.
- ❖ People want some sort of personal involvement in the campaign process.
- ❖ People get upset because their elected representatives are not accessible.
- ❖ Candidates come in all sizes, shapes and descriptions. Some have all the necessary qualifications. Some have none.
- ❖ Never underestimate the news media's importance in any election.

❖ Many voters say that they base their judgment of candidates largely on information they hear, see on the news or read in the papers.

❖ No two candidates, no two campaigns are ever identical.

❖ Marketing is so very important in any campaign. In the business world, an inferior product aggressively sold can often dominate a market.

❖ In business the object is to direct your efforts to make a profit. In all elections the object is to influence the voters to be favorably impressed with the candidate.

❖ If you can get people to say that you talked to them and that they felt you listened and showed interest in their problem, then you are on the right track to success.

❖ Candidates and campaigns are organized to spend money to influence voters. Every political victory is the result of good organization and planning and, above all, a unified effort.

❖ What is the deciding factor when it comes to voting? Is it the candidate's personality, the literature, the opinion of the opposition, or the political philosophy?

Chapter 3

Gathering the Troops

▼

The Best Advice from
U.S. Senator Claiborne Pell of Rhode Island

"I think each politician must develop his or her own strategy.

I have been elected to six terms in the United States Senate with an average vote of 65 percent. I take a great deal of credit for these results by never mentioning my opponent in a critical way.

I also have a seven word motto that I always sought to follow, and that is, 'Translate ideas into events and help people.'"

You've often heard that the early bird gets the worm. That is true of many things, and especially when it comes to a campaign for elective office. It takes time to get your act together, and the sooner you start, the sooner you can start taking care of the many details that need to be addressed. A year in advance is not too early to seek endorsements of key people. Or to do some basic research regarding voting patterns in past elections. Or start asking people for financial support. Or for formulating your positions on important issues that are sure to come up during the campaign. Decide whose support (make a large list) will be important and begin lining them up before any opponent gets to them. You cannot run a race alone.

You hear the term "networking" used these days as though it is a new way of doing things. The truth is, it has been a standard tactic used in politics in this country for a long, long time. It is how a seasoned politico or a potential candidate gets to be known, makes contacts, and finds out what is going on in the political sphere. Many a candidate has first become active in his or her church, PTA, civic clubs, local political organizations, neighborhood group, homeowner association, local charity, etc.

And, in many cases including my own, my wife was a big help with her contacts acquired over the years because of her civic activities. These were very valuable to me in my political races. After all, if you are going to try to become known and liked, you need to be connected with as many people as possible. Never pass up the opportunity to meet new folks.

Be aggressive in some instances, and introduce yourself to others. If you are going to meet people, you can't be shy. So when you can, take the initiative and walk up to people, stick out your hand and say, "Hi, I'm _____." Hopefully they will say their name. If they don't, you need to ask, "What is your name?" Never forget that a person's name is very important. Be sure you get it correct, and do your best to remember it.

You need to know the people who are the voters, the community leaders, the thinking of the people in your area, the issues, and who might or might not support you in a race.

This is what is called forming your own power base. If you have done a good job with that, you will now have the start of what it will take to get elected.

They can't vote unless they're registered, so you need to make sure all your friends and potential supporters are registered to vote. Lists of those who are registered to vote are available through election officials. Check with your local election commissioner or Secretary of State for details. And check party affiliation, of course. Many voters list themselves as nonaffiliated "independent" voters. In many states—in primary elections—these people cannot vote for you if you are a Democrat candidate or a Republican candidate.

And primary elections are so very important, of course. The sad fact is that usually less than 25 percent of all the registered voters vote in primary elections. You need all the votes you can get if you are to win your primary and advance to the general election. Don't put the horse before the cart. I cannot emphasize how important it is to concentrate on the primary election. If you are in a race as one of a number of Democrats, or in a group of Republicans in a primary election, your friends who are registered as independent cannot vote for you in many states. But your Secretary of State in the state capitol is the best source of information regarding election procedures.

You need to form your "Kitchen Cabinet" (some people like to refer to this group as a steering committee, but I prefer the term kitchen cabinet because it's more homey). This is your group of close friends, advisors, politicos who would help guide you and your campaign to victory. After all, that is what should be the ultimate goal of your election efforts. You can't have a major voice in setting policy, or change the way things are done unless you win. Early in the game, put together a list of potential kitchen cabinet members.

Think about what these people can bring to the table. Are they astute politicos? Have they been involved in previous elections? Are they truly dedicated to seeing you elected? Can they help you raise the needed funds for the campaign? Do they have any special skills like knowledge about computers, an organizational wizard who can line up volunteers, street-smart advertising or public relations background, etc.? Start with a list of as many as 40 people, and pare it down. You will find that many, even though they will help you in other ways, will decline to be active in your campaign for a variety of reasons.

The ideal number will vary, but about ten people will give you a pretty good cross section. As the campaign progresses, you will find that some members will drop out and become less interested as they find out that being involved in a campaign takes time and interest. So some folks just won't hang in there.

These members of your kitchen cabinet are expected to lend their names to the campaign for endorsement ads. And you expect them to give the campaign some of their very valuable time, and their money, whether $10 or the limit allowed by law.

Before you invite them to join the group, you need to decide what you hope to accomplish when you all get together. Sure, you will talk about the campaign; that is what you are getting together for. But you need a detailed agenda for every meeting. Have it typed, and give a copy to each person as they arrive so you can systematically cover what needs to be covered. If you don't, it will turn into a bull session, and nothing substantial will get accomplished.

Another thing: you have to respect people's time. Note the suggested invitation. I believe in starting meetings on time and setting definite time limits, and sticking to it. If you don't, a meeting that starts at 7:30 a.m. will have people straggling in at 8 a.m., 8:15, and even 8:30. And when you say the meeting will start promptly at 7:30 a.m. and be over at 9 a.m., you had better mean it.

This type of schedule keeps the discussion on track and keeps your members from getting off on tangents. All should remember that this type of meeting is usually to look at the big picture—not to spend an hour discussing the color of the yard signs. So keep the meeting going. Most of the members will be thankful to you for that if you stick to business. You can discuss the weather, the traffic tie-up, or the latest news items after the meeting is over if you care to stay.

But the hour-and-a-half meeting should be a down and dirty, shirt-sleeve, serious discussion of the matters at hand.

After the first meeting you will need to schedule future get-togethers. Don't have meetings just to have meetings. Busy people's time is very valuable, and you need to respect that if you want to keep them involved.

The typed agenda for the first meeting of your kitchen cabinet that should be mailed to potential members may look like this:

Agenda
Jimmy Jones for Mayor—Kitchen Cabinet Meeting
Saturday, April 16, 19__, 7:30 a.m.-9 a.m.
at Legler Historic Barn, 87th and Lackman

1. Introductions by Jimmy Jones
2. Brief remarks from Jimmy regarding campaign
3. Get organized; select chairperson for campaign

4. Form Steering Committee; discuss each function and responsibility of each member
5. Set time for next general meeting
6. Comments, questions, concerns
7. Adjourn no later than 9 a.m.

Regarding the meeting: during introductions it is very important that everybody gets to know everybody. I like to make out name tags in BIG type so they are readable at a distance. You will probably know each person, but don't assume that everybody else does. Go around the table and ask each person to introduce themselves, and after each introduction, you can say something positive relating to how that person might fit into the campaign. Like, "Last year Betty was the media maven that helped get the bond issue passed!" or, "Joe is the only guy I know who truly knows how those doggone computers work."

The brief remarks should be just that: brief. After all, you are preaching to the choir, and you have much to get done at this meeting. But it would be useful if, in 30 seconds, you would tell everybody enthusiastically why you are running. Tell them how appreciative you are that they are here and are willing to support your efforts. Be straight, be honest and be direct.

In the nicest way you can, ask the members for their time, effort, money, endorsement and advice. They have to understand that there will be plenty of differences of opinions as to how to run the campaign. The ultimate goal is to take the ball across the goal line.

I'm reminded of arguments about such things that took place in my initial campaign for mayor. We had heated discussion about such things as whether the fact that I was an Eagle Scout was worth mentioning on my campaign literature, or if (as some

Gathering the Troops

research indicates) your mail gets opened more often if the stamps are put on crooked vs. put squarely and neatly in the corner of the envelope. The get organized/select a chairperson portion you should have already had worked out.

You should by now have selected a chairperson, and talked to one of the group who you feel is qualified, competent, reliable, trustworthy and that person is willing to accept the position. At the meeting, it is very unlikely you will have people fighting one another to be chairman of the committee. So have one ready. You will find that many people are willing to help, but few want the responsibility of the campaign chairperson.

When it comes to responsibilities of the various Steering Committee members, don't get too complicated. Each function will have one person in charge who can operate individually or with others as a committee.

You'll need a Fund-raising Chairperson to coordinate the big job of raising money for the campaign. As the candidate, you have to realize that you must be very active and involved with this committee especially and its activities if you want the campaign to succeed. It is always tough to get Fund-raising committee members, so I suggest that very early you get that chairperson and committee organized. Let them know that you will be deeply involved with the committee, and you will be happy to get together with them and prospective contributors.

I'll talk about fund-raising in a later chapter, but you need to know that your largest contributors want the candidate (in person or by letter) to ask them for money.

You also have a research committee to review such things as issues involved, the results of past elections, opposition research, etc. Another committee will line up potential speaking engagements for the candidate. In that group is the Scheduler, the **one** person to keep a **master calendar** of commitments for the candidate.

I cannot emphasize how important it is to be coordinated in the ways I've mentioned. The Scheduler shouldn't make any commitments for the candidate until clearing it first. And be careful not to make commitments too far in advance because you will find that Murphy's Law will come into play. As soon as you have committed yourself to one event, the candidate will be invited to a much larger and potentially much more important event at the same time and date. Since you can be at only one place at a time, be sure you're at the right one. And in determining what events to attend, the key is how many potential votes *for me* will be at this event?

Volunteers play an enormous role in any campaign. Thank them over and over. You cannot run a campaign alone, and thank the good Lord that there are people who are willing to help you win.

But in all of this, try not to get too complicated. You can form more committees later if you need them.

An ideal situation for the second general meeting would be to get the group together for an all-day meeting on a Saturday in a hotel room or meeting room somewhere. There the group can kick around all kinds of ideas in a very frank, honest, no-holds-barred, down-and-dirty fashion in an informal manner. It will be a bull session of sorts, but strictly dealing with all the facets of the campaign.

At this meeting, discuss the strengths and weaknesses of the candidate, the strengths and weaknesses of opponents (how to exploit the one and minimize the other), issues and potential issues, the resources available to the campaign...money, time, people, etc.

Oh, yes, as the candidate you need to consider one more key job, someone who would make a good campaign manager. That's the person to run the campaign on a day-to-day basis. Good solid open discussion amongst your Kitchen Cabinet/Steering Committee friends and supporters will solidify the group, and this campaign becomes "their" campaign.

Get Elected, Make a Difference!

Rich Becker, Missouri Senator Kit Bond and son, Sam Bond

Chapter 4

Getting Ready to Run

▼

The Best Advice from
U.S. Senator Phil Gramm of Texas

"I learned from my mother that the way to succeed is to start sooner, work harder and try to know more than anybody else. Losing is a habit, and so is winning. Come to think of it, most of the best advice I ever received came from my mother."

"If you don't run, you can't win!"

As you are getting ready to run, you will truly feel like you're in a fish bowl. You and the members of your family will feel like every move you make is being watched and scrutinized. You have to accept it; it is part of the game. You are going to discover if you don't realize it already, that you can't be thin-skinned and be involved as a candidate.

Your friends will love you, but the opposition will delight in taking verbal shots at you, and so will the media at times. You and your family all have to be prepared, and for the most part there are ways to deal with the situations as they arise, which will be discussed later. You will find, as I have found, that nobody in politics is perfect. We have all made mistakes, done dumb things, made stupid remarks or comments sometime in our past for which we would give anything to retract. But you have to live with them and make the most of it.

Rest assured that your past transgressions are known to the opposition and that they will be brought up during the campaign. We'll talk about this later, but from the moment you decide to run, it is important to watch what you say and do. You need to visualize that any comment or statement to anybody—under any circumstance—any action you take or get involved in (whether a traffic ticket or a local scandal) could end up on the front page of your local paper or on the evening TV news. And that you obviously don't need.

A note to female candidates with children: be on the alert for people who will criticize you for neglecting your family or being a lousy mother for spending your time politicking when you should be spending "quality time" with your children.

A great way to defend yourself is to get your children involved. This is the 1990s, and most people will understand.

Heck, even when I was a kid growing up in St. Louis and my mother was running for committeewoman and my dad was a candidate for Justice of Peace, my brothers and I decorated wagons along with our friends and held a parade around the neighborhood. We stuffed envelopes and put stamps on the envelopes, and we went door to door handing out literature and putting up signs. We were part of the campaign, and proud of it.

A candidate has to be credible. You have to be believed, to gain supporters. Many potential candidates gain credibility by taking a very active part and getting deeply involved in all kinds of clubs and organizations and political campaigns of other candidates. In this way, a person will have some idea of what he or she will be getting into as a candidate.

Taking leadership positions, speaking out on issues, making friends, and letting people know by your actions that you can get things done all help improve your credibility. To be a credible candidate, people need to think of you as a thoughtful and insightful and serious person. After all, people will not support, or vote for, someone they don't believe is serious enough in their quest for public office.

Edward R. Murrow once said, "To be persuasive, we must be believable; to be believable, we must be credible; to be credible, we must be truthful."

The physical health of a candidate is very important. I can tell you from personal experience that campaigning is a grueling task, and you have to take care of yourself. In the heat of the battle, you develop some very bad eating habits. If you smoke, I encourage you to quit, cold turkey, **NOW.**

And watch the booze. Not only from the fact that some people find it offensive for you to smoke and drink, but one too many drinks can get you in a real jam. You don't have to be a "health nut," but you do have to show some good ol' common sense and a sense of moderation in eating and drinking. Your campaigning, going door to door, should take care of the exercise aspect of your campaign.

Your mental health is also very important. I truly believe that the most important attribute a candidate can have is a great attitude. In a campaign, the world can come apart at the seams, but if you have a great attitude, you will survive. Sure, you'll have your setbacks, we all do at times.

I learned a long time ago that I did not have a lock on all the good ideas in the world, and I learned a long time ago that not everybody loves you, or will love you regardless of what you do or say. Accept the fact that we are living in the real world, and get on with your life and your campaign. We live in an imperfect world, and we are all imperfect human beings.

In general, laugh at yourself for the dumb stuff you do or say, and try not to make the same mistake the second time. Nobody's perfect. And don't waste your time dwelling on mistakes. You have a campaign to take care of. Get on with it. And certainly you will find many things that irritate you along the way, so lighten up, and try not to complain too much about this or that. Nobody likes to hear people whining or complaining. Let those irritations roll off you like the proverbial water off a duck's back.

And getting ready to run requires the collection of signatures. In some states, some races, a certain number of names are required before your name can be put on the ballot. And in those states, you will need these signatures before you file. The requirements will vary from state to state and area to area. The names you collect have to be on a specific form or petition. Here again, check with your Secretary of State's office first if you're seeking a state office. They will be able to direct you to the proper source of information. Or contact your county election office if you are seeking a county office, or the city clerk if you are seeking a city office.

The number of signatures required to get on the ballot is usually a percentage of the total vote in the last general election. Here again, this requirement may vary. These are details that must be handled properly. The signatures will have to be of registered voters, and if you are running in a partisan election, may have to be of registered voters of your party. And as you collect them, you need to collect many more than are actually required. That's because many people will sign these petitions (or any petition) just to get rid of you. But they, in fact, live in a different district or aren't even registered to vote.

To give you an idea of why you need plenty of excess signatures, look at a recent petition drive in Harry Truman's old home town, Independence, Missouri. A total of 16,000 signatures were collected, but 48 percent were invalid, and 24 percent of the signers were not registered to vote. And 641 had the wrong addresses, while 77 dead persons "signed" the petition. So you can see there is need for extras.

Start collecting from the people you know, your friends and neighbors and committee members and go on from there. Some people go door to door of registered voters and kill two birds with one stone. That's preferable. But the names can be collected at the mall or in front of the grocery store. Many businesses frown on any kind of political activity on or near their property, so you may get tossed out. But give it a try, and then move elsewhere until you have the names.

For larger areas, you will need volunteers, since the law often requires that certain percentages of the total you collect must be representative of the entire district you seek to represent. So that means getting into a lot of corners in the district.

Computer lists of registered voters are available from election offices and from some political parties, as well as from private sources like Aristotle Industries in various formats from CD's to hard copy printouts.

More about lists later.

Candidate Profile

For starters, you want to become a candidate. You do not consider yourself a politician, and you know nothing about conducting an election campaign. You think of yourself as a citizen who should get involved, because, "I can do a better job than those dummies." You maybe feel like I feel, that I want more of a say in what is taking place. And if you do, then you have to get involved. All of that is a key to a good candidate profile.

But there is more. You don't have to be a millionaire or a lawyer or have a Ph.D. or be a "know-it-all." But you need to be smart enough to analyze yourself in real world terms. Here are some thoughts and ways to help you.

Take some time and carefully document your life—your accomplishments, your education, your family life, your background, all the pluses and minuses. (In any campaign, you will promote your pluses, and your opponent will be sure to tell everybody about your minuses). Get it on paper. Once you do, you will begin thinking about it, and you will find yourself adding items long forgotten, or items you hope people will forget about.

All this information will be used in compiling a candidate profile, a candidate fact sheet, a candidate's statement, a candidate bio (biography) or whatever different people will call it. Regardless, it is your life on paper.

As you go through the campaign, you and your staff will pick from it items to be included when the newspaper wants to know about your background, or the education association wants to have a bio for your talk before their convention or committee. Or your staff can pull out facts relevant to a particular issue for a news release, etc.

Above all, this self-analysis needs to be realistic and brutally honest. This is *not* a fun exercise. Remember that this is for your use, not for distribution to the media or to be seen on the front page of tomorrow's paper. This is not the time to just look for stuff that makes you look good. Sure, it's not fun to talk about skeletons in closets. You can fool everybody else, but you can't fool yourself. You can't be shy about your accomplishments either. Get them down on paper. Now is the time to be totally honest and blow your own bugle.

As you get into the process, think positively. Especially don't be cynical about politics. If the door opens, take advantage of the opportunity. You likely will be welcomed with open arms.

And a word about egos. A candidate must have a strong sense of self-esteem or he or she wouldn't be a candidate in the first place. I know that many people look at a large amount of confidence as a deterrent. But I try to lighten the subject whenever anybody brings up the subject of a big ego by saying something like, "My head is so big it won't fit through the door, but my heart is in the right place," and laugh about it. There is nothing wrong with having an ego. It is how you project it that matters.

More about self-analysis. Consider these things in the process:

- Your accomplishments?
- Your abilities?
- Your greatest assets?
- Your weaknesses?
- Your education?
- Things in your background that will be assets to your campaign?

- ❖ Things in your background that will be liabilities in your campaign?
- ❖ Your family's feelings about your run for office?
- ❖ How will the campaign affect your personal life?
- ❖ How will the campaign affect your business life?
- ❖ If I am elected, what conflicts will I potentially have?
- ❖ What are the major issues as I see them now? And what are my feelings about these issues now? (I say "now," because I think it is smart for a person to always reserve the right to change their opinion about an issue if new information is presented that warrants such a move.)

After you have done the self-analysis, you need to ask your spouse or a close friend or two who will be brutally honest with you for *their* analysis of you. Ask them to do it in private, then compare their opinions with yours. You may find that you see yourself in a diffferent light than others see you.

Preliminary Media Contact

Once you decide to run, you need to start making the rounds of the media. Make a simple phone call in advance to the editor of the paper (or the news director of radio or TV stations) to find out the best time for them for you to stop by and introduce yourself because you are going to be a candidate. This is not only common courtesy, but you probably wouldn't be welcome if you showed up unannounced just at the deadline. Be sure you prepare a one-page fact sheet to leave behind, highlighting the basic facts about yourself: your name, address, age, occupation, education, marital status and some of your leadership positions and accomplishments. Double space it and make it easy to read. For newspapers, bring along a good 8" x 10" or a 5" x 7" black and white photo that you had taken by a professional photographer. They may want to use it. Sometimes they would prefer to have one of their staff take a photo while you are there.

When to Announce Your Candidacy?

There are many ideas of how best to take care of this very important part of a campaign. I'd suggest you check on when other candidates running for the office you are seeking announced in the past. Look up old newspaper clippings at the library. Don't rely on a previous candidate's memory, because it is my experience that they rarely remember accurately.

For a local or statewide race, it is best to announce when you have made up your mind and are pretty sure you can raise the needed money. I believe it is best to be the first person in the race. You scare off some potential opponents, and you will get news coverage in every story about anyone else who announces. Supporters and potential supporters will know it is official. With this announcement you are saying, "I am running!" You will be referred to as the first person to enter the race. I suggest in all your news releases you continue to remind the media of that fact.

I can't emphasize how important it is to line up support early. Many a candidate took his or her time in making the decision and found out that people whom they had counted on for support were already committed to other candidates. You should begin lining up support many months before you even make this announcement.

Don't confuse your announcement with your actual filing for office. When you announce, you hold a news conference. This is called your formal announcement. You call the media, you issue a news release saying you intend to run and give the media information on your background and your plans. Have your announcement at a convenient place and time so it will be in the latest edition of the paper or on the 6 p.m. news. I suggest you find out the best time when you are making the rounds of the media getting acquainted in the weeks prior. The media will be happy to suggest the best time of day and the best day of the week.

Holding a news conference is not the only way to do it. You could make the announcement at a lunch or dinner or even a rally. Whatever, your announcement may be one of the biggest events of the campaign, so make it a big deal for maximum impact and remembrance. One note of caution. Schedule the announcement on a slow news day if possible. I know you don't have control over the unexpected, but *don't* schedule your announcement on the day of major local or national news events if you can anticipate them.

In your news release, be sure to say why you are running because it will be asked of you many times.

More about news conferences and news releases later, but I suggest you put together a media kit for distribution at the news conference, and for distribution to the media who were unable to attend. If someone could not attend, it is important that you deliver the kit to the media immediately after the news conference. This kit should contain, among other things, a news release, a recently taken professional black and white glossy photo (not your high school photo), and a fact sheet/bio. Daily papers, weekly papers and TV all will have some different photo requirements. So as you make the rounds of the media, ask them what works best for them.

The reason to do things this way is for maximum exposure and name recognition. In its simplest sense, when a person goes into the voting booth, you want to be sure that your name is on their mind in a positive way so they will vote for you. That's the bottom line.

When to File?

Sometime after you have made your announcement, you will officially file for office. For some offices, this will mean you will present your filing petitions to the proper election official, fill out the necessary papers and pay the necessary fees. There are no standard procedures from state to state, as well as for counties, parishes, districts and cities. Your Secretary of State's office should be the first stop in finding out about procedures and requirements. After that, I would be sure to contact the county or city election officials. It seems like every election cycle you will hear of people who file for office, only to be disqualified because they did not meet residency requirements or registered using a part-time address rather than their real home address, or never registered to vote, or were purged from the voter registration rolls because they have failed to vote in previous elections. There are strict requirements; make sure you meet them. There are even special requirements for certain offices. The correct information is only a phone call away.

Don't file on the day of the filing deadline. You'll get lost in the shuffle. I know there are some people who talk about running but think it is a smart move to wait until the deadline to file. Sometimes they don't even make an announcement. I don't think much of that idea because I think it is important to make a commitment early, start lining up supporters and money and let everybody know you are a serious candidate. The last-minute strategy diminishes your credibility, and you are thought of as a person who can't make up his or her mind.

Years ago Murray Chotiner, political guru and advisor to many politicians, said that for candidates to be successful, they must be qualified and must have a clean record. What the public doesn't know about the candidate the opposition either knows or will find out and use in the campaign. The candidate must clearly present the issues. You can't talk out of both sides of your mouth, and you can't work both sides of the street. The candidate must stand for something. He must stand for one thing or one basic idea or project that appeals to the voters. And the candidate must be courageous. He must be willing to stand up for what he believes in and put on a fighting tough campaign. Chotiner's words are true—and worth re-reading.

Women in Politics

Some people consider this a touchy subject, but I don't. I've known many women who have run for and served in various offices. I've supported a number of woman candidates with hard work, advice, sweat and money. I've been fortunate to serve with and be good friends of Mayors, City Council members, County Commissioners, State Senators and State Representatives on the local and state level. Many of these elected officials are women. Regardless of what the current feeling is between the sexes, I still believe that women are different from men, and men are different from women. I was amused a year or so ago when the headline on a national magazine announced like it was startling news, "Men and women are different." Of course they are. We do things differently and emotionally handle things differently. So what? Most women I know serving in public office do a terrific job. I've noticed that they are very detail-oriented. The ones who are elected have an interest in a variety of issues and concerns, not just one issue or just "women issues" as some people would have you believe.

The reason I even bring up the subject of women in politics is that I want to make one point. If you have done your homework, have a background of getting things accomplished, a good personality, willing to work hard, and are not a one-issue candidate, then you can win and will get support not only from fellow women, but from plenty of men as well. Sure there will be men who will not support a woman. And there are women who will not support another woman, but it has been my experience in recent times that the criteria over and above all for getting support is having credibility. Sure there are jerks, jackasses, pushy broads and good-ol'-boys that you will run across along the way. But after all is said and done, most voters still will vote for the person whom they feel can best handle the job, period. And that is the way it should be.

As you may have gathered, I'm not in favor of electing women because they are women any more than I favor electing men because they are men. But women who need additional encouragement and money should refer to the list in the back of this book for more information.

Attitude

Approach all problems with the attitude that they can be worked out. To win, you have to really want the job and have fire in the stomach. That is more important than almost any other factor.

Values

You hear so much talk about values these days. When you consider values, remember that voters will look at the candidate's character. And character includes the values of honesty, competence, integrity, hard work, family, home, love, vision, creativity, communication, cooperation, professionalism, accountability and responsibility.

A Few Notes About Leadership

Leadership can be defined with three criteria:

1. The ability to set an agenda
2. The ability to build consensus
3. The ability to take risks

Voters don't have to agree with you all the time. They will admire you for being a person who doesn't mind taking a position and making it known.

When President Carter was at his lowest rating ever, his advisors urged him to lead the country and to concentrate less on governing it. A leader's job, as far as I'm concerned, is to elevate the motives and goals and values of followers by his or her leadership.

Your goal is to be the very best at what you do.

When I was Mayor, I felt progressive leadership had made Lenexa Mid-America's most dynamic community. It is a great place to live, work, raise a family and do business because of caring city government and people-oriented activities. We always felt that although we enjoyed the finest of services and community programs, our goal was always better government, not more government for your money.

Leadership means personally exercising the courage to create an environment that reflects the way you would want to do business. That includes honesty, conviction and devotion.

Listening

Too many politicians spend too much time talking and not enough time listening.

Opportunities

I was raised to believe that we all should be involved and in some way serve our communities. Instead of complaining and moaning and groaning and singing the blues, seize the chance to make a difference. Someone is going to serve in these many offices that set the public policies we all have to live by, and it might as well be you. You have as much common sense as that other person who is running or is now serving in the office you are thinking about. Right? You need to assert yourself. You need to show your strength. The fear of the unknown is always with us. Sure there are roadblocks and barriers, but the road to getting elected you will remember the rest of your life. In a winning campaign, getting there truly is half the fun.

I've personally been in a number of races as the candidate. I've won most of them, but I have lost two of them. In addition, I have worked for a number of candidates and issues. Doing public service is good for the soul. You have to have an interest in making a difference. And believe you can, regardless of your background. Who knows better the day-to-day issues that need to be changed than you? Carefully consider the opportunity to serve. Sure you have business and family obligations. We all do. You need balance. I've always felt that it is amazing what you can do when you really want to, and amazing what you can't do if you really don't want to.

Your Worst Nightmare

Not everybody wins. Only one person can be elected to each position. And that means there will be people who will lose. These are not losers, but people who were beat out by a person who received more votes. It is not easy to accept losing, but in the real world it does happen. I had the misfortune to have surgery for a new heart valve and had double bypass surgery on the day of the primary election that I unfortunately lost. So I know the feeling. Many people never run because they fear losing. Thinking that they might lose the election is the worst nightmare for many potential candidates. Nobody who has any competitiveness likes to lose. I have known all kinds of people who have won elections and who have lost elections. And those who did not win all have survived the ordeal and gone on with their lives. There are those who think it is an embarrassment to lose, but quite the opposite is true. You will gain admiration from neighbors and friends if you put up a good battle because you had the guts to stand up for what you truly believe in. And you will be a much wiser person because of it. It is the greatest growth experience you can have.

Novices in Politics

The traditional method for a person interested in politics to really learn is to join one of the major parties as a volunteer. The experience gained in a local political organization can be the springboard to elective office. Working in a few campaigns can give you a wealth of knowledge about people and an appreciation of what a run for office is all about. Some people bypass the local political party and start on their own. Whichever way you start, you must be identified as a leader. This is best accomplished by meeting people, speaking out on issues of concern and making friends.

Doing Your Homework/Assessing Your Chances

At this stage of your quest for public office, you need to do your homework. It is smart to gather all the facts you can so you can make an intelligent decision. Don't get the idea that being involved in a political campaign and getting elected is easy. There is a lot of hard work and personal sacrifice. You need a hard-nosed assessment of your chances. That is why you need to take an objective look at the factors involved.

- ❖ Things in your background that will be liabilities in your campaign? Your first task is to find out as much about the job you are seeking as possible. If it is a city office, check with the city, if a county office or state office, check with the appropriate election office.
- ❖ Spend time at the local library. Check their clipping files. Ask the librarian about any information they may have on previous elections.
- ❖ Your local newspaper will have clippings covering past elections, the candidates and the issues. If you find clippings of particular interest, be sure to make notes of the dates and page numbers in case you need that information in the campaign.
- ❖ Local newspaper people, editors and reporters have a vast knowledge about past elections, candidates and issues.
- ❖ Your local election office has records of vote totals from past elections for the wards, precincts, districts in which you are interested.
- ❖ Financial reports from past elections, listing contributions and expenditures are available for inspection. Check with your Secretary of State, your county election office and at City Hall. These reports contain valuable information as to who supported whom and with how much.
- ❖ Your local political party has information on party registration and past voting records.

- At City Hall, you can obtain voting records of anyone with a city office. (These records are open to the public.)
- You can check with the Police Department and Sheriff if you want to find out if your opponent has any arrest or criminal record on file.
- Obtain a copy of the election codes from the Secretary of State and review them.

Pre-announcement

Before you announce your intentions to the public in general, your friends, associates, supporters, local politicos and media should all be informed. Obviously, you ask them all to keep the information confidential until the official public announcement. People appreciate that you trust them to keep confidence, and the local paper may even go so far as to print an editorial that might be favorable.

Before you formally announce, make sure you have done the work necessary to be a credible candidate. Winning an election takes effort and expertise. Once you formally declare your candidacy, the public expects you to act like a candidate. And from that moment on, you will be treated like a candidate. You will be asked over and over, "Why are you running for this office?" and "What are your feelings about this?" and "What are you going to do about that?"

You're a Candidate, But Not a Politician

You want to become a member of your City Council, or school board, etc., but you don't know beans about the process of getting elected. Getting elected to public office isn't an impossible dream. Every community is different, every election is different. But there are common factors to most successful campaigns, especially on the local and state level. These are much more personal than a campaign for Congress, as an example. You will need to deal with not only your friends and neighbors, but you need to extend yourself to meet many new people. It's true that a local official is the closest to the people. You can always find him or her. And that officeholder is generally much more in touch with what is going on locally and easier to get hold of if there is a problem that needs immediate attention.

A big television or radio campaign for a local election would seem overly ambitious. Not only would it be a waste because the commercials would reach many people outside the candidate's district, but it could be perceived that the candidate is trying to buy the election. In these local elections the key is to contact those who would vote—one to one. And your campaigning should put emphasis on putting your best foot forward all the time.

Plus you need to be informed. My first attempt at public office was an eye-opener. I became very involved in school issues in attempting to have a new school built for our children. For two years I attended every public meeting of the local school board. What an excruciating experience that was! I learned so many things that I really didn't care to know about. I sat through long, long discussions that went late into the night. I ran for an at-large seat on the board and was soundly defeated. It was my first try at public office. It was a fantastic educational experience that I will never forget.

I encourage you to attend meetings of the public body you are interested in so you get a feel for what is involved. It won't take long to get an idea about the issues.

Non-candidates

Not every candidate in every election is in the race to win. Some run on a lark; some run so they have a stage to vent their anger about an issue; some run because it is a way to get free news coverage; some run because it is a way to get their name in the paper; and some run just to give the other candidate a bad time. These people are non-candidates. Their name is on the ballot, but their chances of winning are very slim. Thank goodness!

Power

Once you are elected, you will be setting public policy—that is, the laws by which the citizens will be expected to live. You and your fellow elected officials will be making decisions that will affect others. Depending on the position you are elected to, you will be setting speed limits, deciding who gets contracts, what buildings shall be built, what taxes will be raised, etc. That is power. Some people do run for public office to attain power. Henry Kissinger once said, "Power is the ultimate aphrodisiac."

Filing

I once asked a friend who was very qualified why he didn't run for a certain public office. His wife was not real keen on politics or his involvement in politics. He said, "I'd like to, but if I file, she will file—for divorce."

Special Interest Groups

You hear a lot about special interest groups. Many consider them a scourge—only concerned about big business or big organizations that have a lot of money and power and want still more. Right?...Wrong.

Be careful about the term special interest group. That can also mean a group of parents who band together and go to City Hall to ask for a stop sign on a dangerous corner or a group of citizens who want the city to help promote an art fair. Without special interest groups, many important concerns would be overlooked and not get brought to the attention of elected officials.

Resources You Will Need

If you are to be successful, you must use the resources available to you very carefully—Money, People and Time.

Getting Ready to Run

Making Promises

Every candidate makes promises—actual or implied. You're better off if you limit your campaign promises to the discernible major aspirations of the voting public. Obviously the candidate who over-promises and is elected will suffer the wrath of the electorate for not being able to accomplish all that was promised. It is not possible to be all things to all people. You have to resist the temptation to promise every voter what you think that voter wants. Sometimes people want you to promise to vote *for* something, and sometimes they want you to promise to vote *against* something. Be very careful. Don't over-promise. The best plan of action (not everybody will love you for it) is to agree to study the matter, bring it before a committee and hold hearings on it. But as soon as you say, "Yes, you have a good point, I agree with you and I will do that," you have a potential problem on your hands. You'd better mean it and deliver. You will find that voters have short memories of the good stuff you do and very, very long memories of the bad things.

Whatever you do, be sure the promises you make fit the expectations of the people to whom you make them.

First Position

The name at the top of the ballot is said to be worth up to an eight percent advantage over the names below it. In many races, that can mean the difference between winning and losing. In some states the first person to file gets the first position. I have seen people representing candidates sleeping in line outside election headquarters on the day that official filing for public office begins so they can be the first person to register for a particular office and get the first position on the ballot.

In some states and communities, the first slot is drawn by lot, and in some it is automatically rotated from polling place to polling place so all candidates for an office have a chance for their name to be at the head of the list. Here again, check with the Secretary of State for the formula in your state.

Chapter 5

Organization/Steering Committee

▼

The Best Advice from
Congressman Mike Parker of Mississippi

"Work hard, always tell the truth, have one position and stick to it (whether you are speaking to a group that supports your position or not), and most importantly, realize that without direction and guidance from God, you will never amount to anything."

Headquarters

In very small campaigns you can operate out of your kitchen or garage or basement. For a citywide campaign or larger, you will probably need a larger space.

Try to find a place that is in a central location, has parking, and if in a city is close to bus routes and away from a crime-ridden area that would keep volunteers away.

You should be able to make a deal with someone you know in the real estate business for a place. For one of my campaigns we rented a house near the downtown area very inexpensively, and in another instance, a store front in a shopping center was secured. Look around, find the ideal spot, and talk to the owner. You may have to clean the place up and throw out tons of trash or whatever, but it can be made comfortable. Gather some volunteers together for a campaign headquarters cleanup day. You'd be surprised how many people show up with brooms and buckets to help. You can take most places and turn them into a presentable headquarters with a little elbow grease.

Don't spend a lot of money on your headquarters unless you're loaded with dough. You don't need luxury. In fact, some of the fondest campaign memories I have are from the house we cleaned up and used in my first campaign for Mayor.

You can beg and borrow furniture and folding tables, desks, file cabinets and chairs. Campaign signs can be put on the windows, and campaign signs, motivational posters, charts, lists of job responsibilities, campaign photos and check lists can be put on the wall. You'll need a cooler for soda and maybe some beer and coffee. Remember you're not running a restaurant.

It won't take long after you are in your headquarters before you will find out what you need in the way of furniture and equipment. Order your phones as soon as you can. They take time to get installed, and you want them in operation the day you move in.

Campaign Equipment and Supplies

A campaign office these days will incorporate more than the traditional equipment like tables and chairs, paper and pens and a coffeemaker and cooler. It will have a copier, a fax machine, cellular phones, pagers and, of course, a computer with a laser printer.

The candidate and the campaign manager will have cellular phones in their cars and pagers on their belt. These days, if there is a statewide campaign, many candidates will use a mobile home as their moving office.

Stationery

Yes, you will need stationery. But before you order it, decide on the art work, the design, the colors and the theme of the campaign so everything is coordinated. Your campaign will look amateurish if the artwork is one color on your stationery, a different color on your brochure and still a different color on your yard signs.

When you do order, don't order a 25-year supply. The campaign will be over and done with in a few months at most, so don't go overboard.

Along the left border you should list the campaign chairman and all the members of your Steering Committee.

Campaign Manager

Who will be your campaign manager is probably the single most important decision you will make. Obviously, you should get the best manager you can. You need a competent campaign manager, a person who has a good knowledge of local politics and the local area, a person who can direct and inspire, a person with good management and good people skills, a person who can get done what needs to get done under the pressure of a campaign, a person who is 100 percent loyal to you. Then you can go about campaigning and know that most of the details of the election are being taken care of.

The campaign manager will plot and plan and organize, troubleshoot, be sensitive to issues, represent you in important negotiations, spend campaign money and make sure the stuff of a campaign gets done. There are volunteers to put to work, canvassing of neighborhoods to do, contributions to deposit, and events to bring in other people to get involved in the campaign, advertising to buy, mailings to get out, papers to read, radio and TV reports to hear and see, and a thousand and one other things. You need to spend your valuable time on the street and on the phone campaigning. You have to be able to maximize the time you spend out with the voters instead of worrying if the details of the campaign are being taken care of. You notice that I did not say "little details," because there are very few "little details." They are all important.

As an example, in every election campaign I have ever been associated with, there have been personality differences and conflicts between people associated with the campaign. The manager needs to deal with these situations immediately before they disrupt the campaign.

The campaign manager has the ultimate responsibility for anything that is done in the candidate's name. The manager must make the candidate look good. He or she must represent your best interests and be a person you can count on. It has to be someone you're comfortable with intellectually and emotionally. The manager and the candidate meet frequently, discuss things honestly and openly, and they stay as close as a phone call or a beep on a pager.

The candidate and the manager need to have an understanding from the very beginning regarding decision-making. As the campaign progresses, critical decisions need to be made, often on the spur of the moment. If the candidate is going to micromanage the campaign and make every decision regardless of how large or small, then the manager is not being used effectively. The manager needs to be extremely honest and straight with the candidate, and not a "yes" person. It is easy to give the candidate all the good news of a campaign. But some people are reluctant to tell the candidate about the bad news. I assure you that there is always some bad news that comes along that needs to be brought to your attention.

The candidate should be more concerned about the big picture and should not have to be burdened with all the many details. In most campaigns, the manager handles the day-to-day operation and confers with the candidate on matters of strategy. I know that sounds like a pretty loose arrangement, but you have to be flexible. You cannot put on paper all the what-ifs. You have to have trust in your manager that good judgment will prevail. It has always worked well in my campaigns to have the manager taking care of the internal things, and I would be free to spend all my time on the outside—things like going to coffees, going door to door, talking to organizations, etc. You and your campaign manager must be on the same frequency philosophically or you will be heading for trouble.

The manager may have to fire incompetent workers. Now you ask how can you fire a volunteer? You can't really, but you can give them other duties that will do less harm to the campaign. In all campaigns, opportunities arise to move people around. It is the responsibility of the manager to be on top of the situation and take immediate action where necessary. The other workers know who is not doing their part, and if it continues, it can cause serious morale problems. And that you don't need.

For a very small election, you can be your own manager. I was when I ran for the City Council. But when I ran for Mayor, I needed and had an outstanding manager and kitchen cabinet. Frankly, how big your campaign is should be in relation to how big the position you are seeking is. A very expensive-looking or sounding campaign looks and sounds out of place if you are running for a seat on the City Council. Beautiful four-color brochures and TV and radio spots might give the impression that you are trying to buy the seat and are out of place as a candidate.

Campaign Money

In every campaign there are thousands of reasons to spend money. You will find, if you don't already know, that everybody is an expert when it comes to campaigns and what is necessary to win. And every idea and scheme costs money. It is the job of the campaign manager to be absolutely hard-nosed, cold-blooded and tight as can be with the campaign money. One reason is to be sure your maximum impact is at the end of the campaign. But you must also resist the temptation to buy from every person who walks in the door, calls on the phone, or is suggested by one of your volunteers. Study, ask questions and be very frugal. Think long and hard before you spend a dime. Make every penny count.

Each Campaign Is Different/
Each Campaign Is the Same

Your campaign will lose some people as the campaign progresses because you will have people who lose interest because you "wouldn't listen to their suggestions." If in your best judgment the idea has merit, go for it. If not, in your most diplomatic way possible, you need to let the volunteer know why. But be prepared; you *will* lose people.

No two campaigns are exactly the same. The candidates are different, the issues change, but the overall objective is the same—to win. Period.

Party Organization

Your local party organization can help you in your campaign to differing degrees. Some organizations are strong and have resources like time and people and money to help. For the most part, though, they are more a source of information. Don't count on them for much, if any, money.

Contacts

Don't ever pass up an opportunity to meet people. It is amazing how you find out that one person knows someone you know. And because of that association, they will become a supporter because, "If Betty supports you—and I have a lot of respect for Betty—I'll support you."

As you meet people, it is important to find out what they do and get an idea of what organizations they belong to. With that information, you can ask them to introduce you to others and widen your support and friends.

Many candidates who are new to politics never get used to asking people for help and asking people for money. Asking people for money has never been a problem for me because I've been in sales positions all my life. But you don't have to have a sales background to ask people for help. Most are flattered to be of help to your campaign. Many potential volunteers and supporters never get involved because nobody asked them to help. I know that sounds crazy, but it is the truth.

Organizational Structure/Chart

A comprehensive organizational structure is essential. In a campaign many individuals are involved. You need to be sure all their talents are used efficiently and effectively. Don't try to be a "one-man band." You cannot do the campaign alone. If you think you can, you are going to find yourself sadly mistaken.

Your resources of time, money and people must all be put to good use. As an example, in local and state elections you need to recruit and put as many volunteers as possible to work. They have an interest; they want to contribute; they don't cost you anything; they can influence friends to become supporters; they can recruit still more volunteers. They are necessary if you are going to have a community organization that can reach all of your target voters.

Candidate's Spouse

This person plays a critical role. Hopefully the spouse will play an active, visible role attending functions with the candidate, standing in for the candidate, making phone calls, thanking people, working at headquarters. Just the fact that the spouse is interested, involved and unselfishly supports your candidacy is a boost to you and your volunteers. They can see that the person closest to the candidate cares enough to be involved. If the spouse is never around, campaign workers will wonder why.

Campaign Chairman (Chairperson for those who want to be politically correct)

This person should have the most prestigious name you can come up within your community. But this person is expected to be a member of the kitchen cabinet and one of the steering committee members doing his or her part for the campaign far beyond just lending a name to the campaign.

Overall Campaign Plan

There are a thousand ways to organize a campaign. They all have their pluses and minuses. The best method I have found is to have a small group of individuals, called the kitchen cabinet/close advisors/executive committee/lieutenants (whatever you want to call it, I'll call it the kitchen cabinet) to put together the strategy in conjunction with the campaign manager. This is the final decision-making group. Each member of the kitchen cabinet would also be expected to be a member of the steering committee and be responsible for a task. They, in turn, ask other qualified individuals to serve on the steering committee as either committee heads, or individually to take on and be responsible for the many important tasks of a campaign.

It is important to realize that some of these tasks require day-in and day-out attention, while others can be completed in spurts. This plan should be in writing. And it should be confidential because of the sensitive material it would contain. The campaign plan should be written by the campaign manager in conjunction with the candidate and the members of his kitchen cabinet/closest advisors. The charges of the various members of the steering committee, as outlined in the campaign plan, would be made available to them. But the document itself should be kept under wraps for obvious reasons.

Organizational Chart

The kitchen cabinet will consist of the candidate's closest advisors and the campaign manager. It will be their responsibility to plan the campaign and the overall campaign strategy.

The Steering Committee

You are judged by the company you keep!

The steering committee, made up of close advisors, supporters and specially talented individuals from all walks of life, is charged with carrying out the pieces of the campaign plan. One person should be responsible for each task. That person is accountable and responsible for their duty—as outlined in the written campaign plan. Some of these tasks will be done by a committee, but still one individual should have the responsibility to see that they are accomplished. It works best if every one of these members feels a part of a team. We all operate and think differently and go about getting things done differently. So it is important that the campaign manager not try to micro-manage every person and every activity. That being said, all steering committee members report to the campaign manager, who has the overall responsibility of making sure the campaign plan is carried out.

You need very clear lines of authority. People like autonomy. The campaign manager needs to spell out clearly in writing the exact duties of each committee or task, and be sure that they do not overlap. Because if you don't, you will have the troops nipping at one another.

How detailed your organization is will naturally depend on how big your campaign is, which is determined by how big the office is that you are seeking. A race for Governor would have more committee heads. A campaign for City Council or State Representative would have one individual in charge of a group of tasks.

Periodic meetings need to be called by the campaign manager of all steering committee members to keep everybody up to speed, and to occasionally head off dissension among the troops. It is not unusual for members to differ on one or two issues. That's par for the course. But if a person is in total disagreement with the candidate on the issues, you need to ask that person to resign from the committee, because he or she will do nothing more than continually poison the well. And that you do not need.

An individual steering committee member should be specifically in charge of one or more of the following responsibilities:

Absentee voters	Office manager
Advertising	Phone bank
Advance men and women	Polling/surveys
Canvassers	Press secretary
Computer/data processing	Publicity
Direct mail/mailings	Registration
Election day activities	Research
Field supervisor	Scheduler
Fund-raising	Speaker's bureau
Headquarters	Special projects
Issues	Treasurer
Legal advisor	Volunteers
Literature preparation	Voter lists
Literature/yard sign distribution	

Teamwork

Teamwork is so very important. I was reminded of that recently as I drove by a new home under construction on a warm and windy day. The windows of the house were open, and you could see workers inside putting up wallpaper. Outside a worker on a tractor was dragging the lawn prior to putting down sod. Unfortunately, the dust was going in the windows. Everybody was doing their job, but they weren't working together. If you are going to have a successful campaign, one thing you need is for everybody to work together as a team.

Organization/Steering Committee

Consultants

There are consultants and there are consultants. For a small campaign I doubt if you will need one. But for larger races, you may want to use their services. First you and the rest of your kitchen cabinet need to decide what your campaign lacks and what can be acquired with the use of a consultant. Consultants are available for a price to do any and all facets of a campaign, from polling to research to direct mail to publicity to fund-raising, etc. They can even come in and completely take over and run your campaign. They are specialists. If you think you will need any of their services, you need to start shopping and asking a lot of questions of them and of people who they have done work for in the past. Just be sure to get what you pay for because you have to justify the cost of hiring one.

    Some people refer to them as campaign doctors because they are often called in to assist a campaign that is not going well. Frankly, in sick campaigns it is sometimes advantageous to have an outsider analyze what you are doing wrong.

    A while back I was a candidate for Governor of Kansas. As word spread of my candidacy, I began getting calls from all over the country from consultants who wanted to work on my campaign. I believe a significant number of them couldn't find Kansas on a map. Their approach was that if a campaign was successful in New York or Ohio, then it would be successful in Kansas. Maybe so, maybe not. Sure, there are some universal truths regarding campaigns such as are outlined in this book, but I would feel much more comfortable working with a consultant who is familiar with the people in my own part of the country.

The Campaign Manager (Additional Thoughts)

The person running the show, keeping all the players on track and the campaign going full speed ahead toward victory is the campaign manager. A good one settles squabbles (and you will have them in every campaign), is the hatchet man or woman if necessary, and is tough when it comes to spending precious campaign resources, especially money.

The manager has to do a lot of the dirty work, and the candidate must stay out of it. The candidate must maintain a pleasant, positive image. Being a manager is a tough job, with a million details. And you have a lot to be thankful for if you have a good one.

While the candidate and the campaign manager work very closely together on the campaign, the final word must be that of the candidate. And a good campaign manager will have you thinking of him or her as a slave driver by the last days of the campaign.

Chapter 6

Campaign Strategy and Tactics

***The Best Advice from
Congressman Don Young for All Alaska***

"Always stand up for what you believe. In politics, the temptation to waver is great, but the strongest willed politician will be true to the people he/she represents and most importantly to him/herself."

The strategy is your battle plan spelled out in detail, and the tactics are designed to carry out your plan.

Make no mistake about it, the object is to win! Just how you do it will depend on a number of factors. It helps to have a strategy that has been well thought out.

Here are *some* of the things that you need to consider in planning your strategy: (not listed in any particular order)

- ❖ What will be the two or three central issues in the campaign?
- ❖ How can these issues be used to help me?
- ❖ Why am I running in the first place?

- Who are my friends and allies who will support me?
- Can I get prominent individuals to endorse me?
- How am I going to publicize myself and the issues?
- Who will be opposed to me?
- How can I best neutralize my opposition?
- Where will my financial support come from?
- Who are the best people to serve on my kitchen cabinet?

As I said before each campaign is different. Different candidates, different issues, different situations. Be sure you study the forest before you study the trees. You need to have a good idea of the big picture before you start worrying about all the little pieces.

As a candidate you need to put forward a broad agenda, a grand strategy. People want realistic, fair solutions to problems. You can't be all things to all people; that is why you need a plan and you must rely on it. You need to target identifiable groups with a targeted message.

Politics is like laying bricks. Thousands of small actions go into the building of a winning campaign. Successful, well-thought-out campaigns have a sharply-honed, clear, focused, single, central idea. Along with one theme, one slogan needs to be sold to the electorate over and over and over and over.

There is no right way to run a winning campaign. But a universal strategy covers these points:

1. You have to find out who votes.
2. You have to identify who's for you and how to reach them.

3. You have to identify who's not for you.

4. You have to identify who is undecided.

5. You try to convince the undecided to vote for you, especially in the last days of the election because this is the vote that really makes the difference in most races.

6. You have to be sure that the voters who are for you get out and vote.

As an old-time politico told me once, "If the candidate sends the right messages to the right people in the right ways, that candidate will win."

Posture

An important step in developing a strategy is to determine the posture you should take. In this election are you the challenger or the incumbent? Your strategy will be different in each case.

Remember, voters select candidates who think like they do on *most* issues. So candidates would do well to emphasize the many ways on which they and the voters agree.

As you progress through the campaign and deal with the many things that are part of a campaign, never forget that votes determine the winner. Winners are not determined by the number of news releases, or the number of mailings, or the percentages in the polls, or the advertising budget. How many votes you get determines the winner.

During a campaign, you will make mistakes. Two common mistakes many candidates make are: (1) Relying solely on the advice of people who are already for them and (2) worrying about people who are already against them. When you do these things, you lose sight of your target vote, the people who haven't made up their minds yet.

As a *challenger*, you need to be aggressive. You need fire in the belly. If you are in this race to win, you need to talk about yourself and what you can do. You run on what you're going to do, not on what you've done. The question is, what are you going to do? There are differences between you and your opponent. Never think that losing is okay—even if you think your opponent is a good person. If that is your feeling, you are wasting your time and the time of all your friends and supporters.

If there was a solid reason to get in the race, then you must talk about why the opponent needs to be replaced by you.

It is not simple to beat an incumbent, but it can be done and is done all the time. I beat an incumbent who had served two terms as Mayor. It wasn't easy, but I did it. Or rather, we did it—I had an outstanding group of supporters.

An incumbent on the local and state level has much better access to the media and the stories and the headlines than you have as a challenger. During that person's term of office, he or she had a large number of opportunities to be with the public. And these many meetings give the incumbent plenty of chances to let your constituents know about all the good things he or she has been doing in their behalf. That should have produced news and news stories.

As the challenger you have to overcome the advantage that the incumbent has. The first thing that you can attack is the voting record of the incumbent. All public officials in office have voted on a wide range of subjects. And I know from my own experience that when you vote for something, usually half the people are happy, and half the people are unhappy with the way you voted. That is just the way it is. So you need to carefully research the incumbent's voting record. If you do, you will find all kinds of things on which to challenge him or her.

In politics, the smart rule is to challenge the incumbent on their voting record, but not on their personal life.

And pick your fights carefully. Regardless of who you are running against, they must have done some good over the years. Don't give the impression that everything they did was wrong because, as they say, even a clock that is not working is correct twice a day. You'll be accused of sour grapes, and that is not what you need. What you need is to find a few (two or three) significant items in the incumbent's voting record that the voters can relate to and are not happy with, that you talk about over and over. Or maybe you can talk about his not being accessible. You need to hit a soft spot in your opponent's armor—and get him to react.

Occasionally candidates will attack city hall or the state capitol rather than attack the opponent. They will try to establish themselves as a friend of the taxpayer who is tired of the way things are going. Since generally there are not real specifics mentioned, the perception is left that the opponent is either a cause of the mess or will be right at home in it.

The biggest advantage you have as a challenger is the fact that you have no public voting record to attack, but the incumbent does.

You need to neutralize the opposition. Pull the financial reports from previous elections and find out who gave money to whom. Make a special list of those people and mail to them frequently and tell them about your accomplishments.

Those who have contributed significant amounts are people whom you should contact personally and get to know.

As an *incumbent* running for reelection, you need to be sure that your record is one that you can vigorously defend if attacked. There are always at least two sides to every story, and you need to be sure you tell your story the way you want it told, rather than the way your challenger portrays it. Don't beat yourself. Document your promises from the last election. Research your own record. You'll find it is probably much better than it's being portrayed by your opponent. Plus you should have close contact with the voters during your term.

An important key to reelection as an incumbent is name identification (name ID) and the ability of your constituents to identify something positive you have done as an incumbent. It is rare for a candidate with good name identification tied to a positive accomplishment to get blown away in an election.

Campaigning is a learning process. As a candidate I had the personal experience of being invited to events where, upon arriving, I discovered that every person in attendance was already committed to one of the other candidates. Think out where you can spend your campaigning time most productively. You will get smarter as the campaign progresses, and you will pick your places much more carefully.

People like to know that they can find you when they need you or want to talk to you. I have personally always made it a practice to make sure my home and work phone numbers were always listed. Don't ever let the voters feel that you have lost touch with them. You were elected first to represent these voters, and it is critical that you never take your eye off that purpose.

Constituent service is extremely important. Some politicos consider it more important than anything else you do as an elected official. Your constituents want to be able to talk about their problems and concerns. If you don't have the answer, don't tell them, "That's somebody else's bailiwick." They expect you to help them resolve their problem.

I remember sitting in our congressman's office in Washington one time, and he told me that I would be amazed at the number of times people call him regarding their local streets, barking dogs, etc. I know from the many calls, letters and chance meetings at events that people expect you to help them, and I'm happy to do my best. People appreciate that. Sometimes in public office you get so close to it that you think everybody knows about the workings of government. That's not true. Your job is to simplify matters for your constituents. They will not forget your graciousness.

When all else fails, work hard and do a good job for your constituents. Build good name identification, establish good media contacts, identify yourself with at least one very positive accomplishment, identify voters and turn out your voters, win plenty of visibility for yourself and your campaign on election day, and you should be in pretty good shape to be reelected.

Repetition

When your message is clearly defined and you start talking about it, it is absolutely critical that you hammer that message home over and over. Often people in your campaign say, "Gee, don't you think we ought to change that message? I'm sick of hearing it." I spent 30 years in radio and television advertising, and I can tell you that I have heard that scenario a thousand times. The truth is, when you as a candidate or an advertiser are sick of hearing a particular commercial message, that's when "Betty

Smith on 83rd Street" is hearing it for the very first time. As an advertiser or a candidate, you get too close to it. And as a candidate, you are delivering the same identical message over and over, day after day. I know it gets tiresome and boring but, for the most part, you are delivering that message to people over and over for the very first time. Keep it up. Your supporters are anxious to hear your commercials and see your ads, and they will see all of them. That is why they tire of them so quickly. But you have to remember that in the real world, nobody (except for your real supporters) gets up in the morning and says, "I can't wait to hear or see candidate Jones' ad."

Appeals

For the hostile voter, you need to be persuasive. Agree with anything you can. Then answer with facts and logic, point by point. I want to point out something that you will learn in a campaign if you are not already aware of it. In all my years of campaigning I have found that it is essentially a waste of time, effort and energy to argue with someone as you campaign. Some people have plenty of time on their hands and love to argue. And they will take the opposing view, regardless of what you say. If you want to paint the wall blue, they want to paint it green. You are not going to win them over. After all, how many candidates do you know of over the years who got 100 percent of the vote? It is best to say to the person, "Well, it looks like we are just going to have different viewpoints on that issue, but thank you for your thoughts," and move on. Your time is too valuable to waste on a person who is probably not going to vote for you anyway.

The political campaign time frame allows no spare time to educate people on the fine points of all the issues. If you want to educate people, open a school. Otherwise, you have to settle on just highlighting the issues to an interested voter.

You need to find people who are undecided either because they don't know you or the basic issues. Those are the people you need to tell about yourself and your ideas and plans for the future.

For the voters who are uncommitted, listen to their concerns, agree where you can and present your ideas in a friendly manner. And don't get too windy. A person doesn't want to hear a 20-minute dissertation.

Collecting Names

Early on and continuing throughout your campaign, you need to collect names of people you meet who show interest in supporting you. Ask business people for their business card, write down citizens' names as you go door to door, or make a special note on the voter list printout that you carry as you go door to door. This is an extremely valuable list to have to use for fundraising, for volunteers, and after you are elected. These are special people with whom you want to stay in touch. They will be wonderful for bouncing ideas off of, and to get a feel on how well you are doing in serving the people.

Defining the Race/Defining the Issues/ Defining the Opponent

You need to define the race. Be prepared to stand up and say, "This is what I believe, and this is what the other guy or gal believes." That's not negative campaigning; that is setting the issues.

By the same token, be prepared to respond very quickly if your opponent misrepresents your positions or beliefs in any way. No charge your opponent makes should be treated as so preposterous nobody will believe it.

Don't let your opponent set the agenda. Establish it yourself and stick to it. Choose your issues to run on and stick to them. Every attempt by your opponent to pull your campaign off course should be promptly and forcefully met with whatever it takes to get your campaign back on track. Don't fight HIS battles, fight YOUR battles.

Negative Campaigning

Negative campaigning works. What you need to understand is how "negative campaigning" is defined. Any factual, documentable comment or vote dealing with the opponent's public record is perfectly legitimate to use in the campaign.

The thing you are trying to do is create doubts about the capability of your opponent.

Attacks

You don't like mudslinging. Right! Well, I don't either, but a well-documented exposé based on truth and fact is okay and essential.

All kinds of studies have been made trying to figure out why people vote the way they do. One of the best explanations I have ever heard is that voters in general don't vote FOR something, they vote AGAINST something.

Political consultants know that it is easier and more effective to get people stirred up and angry about an issue or candidate than it is to inspire them to vote for a candidate because he or she is a good person with a good program.

Attacks must always be answered. If you are attacked, you must respond swiftly and forcefully to the charge. If you don't, you basically have agreed that the unanswered charge is correct. That will be the perception of the electorate. Leave no shot unanswered. Most people believe that any shot that goes unanswered must be true. If the charge is true, use political jujitsu. Get it out in the open and, as some people say, hang a lantern on it, admit it, then present your side of the issue.

How you respond tells the voters something about how the candidate would respond to a crisis. As a candidate, you should never let your opponent "define" you or set the agenda for the campaign discussion. That is why you need to be prepared and be aggressive from the start.

If a question has been raised publicly about your personal background, you need to address the issue personally.

Note: Not everybody agrees that this is the way to handle attacks. Some maintain that it is best to ignore the attack, let the smoke clear, and maybe answer it later. By talking about it, you give the attacker credit for taking the initiative, and this in turn only exacerbates the situation that you would just as soon let die. As I said before, there are many ways to run a campaign and many decisions to make. You need to use your best judgment on this one based on the situation and the issue. If you have the ammunition to blast back, do it. That will make your opponent think twice about attacking you next time.

If You Are Going to Attack

- ❖ Attack your opponent's qualifications.
- ❖ Attack your opponent's record in office—his or her official votes.
- ❖ Always make certain you can back up any attack with facts.
- ❖ Consult with your legal advisor before you launch a major attack.
- ❖ Don't attack on something that could backfire and get your opponent sympathy votes because you "crossed the line."
- ❖ Never attack a candidate for being too old. Sympathetic senior citizens like me will never let you get away with that.

How Do You Deal with Problems:

How you look at problems and deal with them tells a lot about you. A friend reminded me of the story that was going around when air pollution became a big problem and Congress talked about clean air standards. U.S. car makers hired 500 attorneys while the Japanese hired 500 engineers.

Ask

Ask people for advice. Ask people for help. You'll be amazed at how positive a response you will get. But you have to ask.

Ask for favors. Someone once told me, "If you want to make friends, let someone do you a favor."

Emotions

Voters are guided by four important emotions:

- ❖ Fear
- ❖ Anger
- ❖ Frustration
- ❖ Hope

Elections are won or lost on emotions, not on logic.

Values

The voters' values are more important than the candidates' values. Each voter has values and, as a candidate, you had better value his values or at least appreciate them if you have any hope of getting that vote.

Believe in What You Say and What You Stand For

Stand tall and act like a winner—and know what you are talking about. Set an example, be a gentleman or a lady, and set a higher standard.

Primary Election Strategy

Because one political party or the other is so dominant in some areas of the country, a primary election victory can be tantamount to victory in the general election.

You will need to do plenty of work to get people excited about a primary election. The sad truth is that voters seldom know or care much about the candidates in local primaries. And only a small number of the eligible party voters bother to vote. A strategy that has been used successfully is to go after as many nonvoters as you can and get them to register with your party and then get them to the polls to vote. You should be able to get voter lists that contain voter history. That is, who voted in what elections, and what party they belong to.

Primaries are supposed to be about emphasizing differences between the candidates but are never supposed to shatter the party unity that will be necessary to elect the nominee of the party selected in the primary.

A Primary campaign and a General Election campaign are two quite different and quite distinct campaigns. Never forget you have to win the pennant before you can win the World Series.

General Election Strategy

Don't take anybody for granted. Nobody wants to be taken for granted. Don't assume a person is for you, supports you, and will vote for you. Look them in the eye and ask for their support and their vote. They will then realize you are serious and appreciate your taking the time to ask them. Many a candidate has lost because he or she was so interested in finding new voters that they forgot to actually ask their old friends and supporters for support this time.

Marketing

When you run for office, you have to market yourself. Marketing includes selling. It is everything you do to promote yourself.

The voter wants to be sure you can handle the job. He or she feels that three of the most desirable and important attributes you can have based on your demonstrated hands-on experience are:

- ❖ Strong Leadership
- ❖ Trustworthiness
- ❖ Good judgment

Twelve Good Rules on Selling Yourself to the Voters

1. As Dale Carnegie used to say, talk to people in terms of *their* major interests.

2. In speaking to groups, don't get too windy. "Tell 'em what you're going to tell 'em, tell 'em, and then tell 'em what you told 'em." Then sit down.

3. Talk to the voters in their language. Don't try to use "hi-falutin" terms or political acronyms. Make your talk and conversation good, clean and down to earth.

4. Smile a lot and, on a hot day, sweat a lot. People like to see politicians sweat.

5. Not everybody loves you, so keep your cool if somebody tries to get under your skin.

6. Send personal notes to people you meet on the campaign trail.

7. (A favorite of mine) Carry a small 35mm camera in your pocket and take lots of pictures. When you have them developed, send the photo to the person. They will absolutely love you for it. Over the years, I have taken thousands of photos and sent them out. Sure it costs money, but it is a great way to develop a reputation.

8. Try very hard to remember the names of the people you meet.

9. If a person has a concern they want to discuss, get their name and phone number, and be sure to contact that person later. Your word has to be good.

10. Be visible. Be at all the community events either working in a charity booth or doing something of value to make the event a success. And while you're there, get around, shake hands,

and greet as many people as you can. You're running for office; this is no time to be shy.

11. With every person you meet, make sure to get a line or two in about the campaign, and how you are running because you are fed up with XXXX, or that you want to clean up that mess at City Hall, etc.

12. And always be sure you ask them for their vote. Many a person did not vote for a particular candidate because he or she took the voter for granted and didn't open up their mouth and say, "I'd appreciate your vote on August 3rd!"

What to Say, What Not to Say

Never, but never, say or put anything on paper that you would be embarrassed to see on the front page of the local paper or on the 6 p.m. TV news. I don't care what the reporter says about this or that being "off the record." Remember Connie Chung and Newt Gingrich's mother. Be forewarned. I've always operated on the principle that I don't have any secrets, but I am still careful what I say and write.

Substance and Style

The public wants to see public signs and signals from you. Many a good candidate has gone down the tubes because he or she tried to substitute substance for style. How you act in public and how the public sees you in public is as important as what you say. The outcome of many elections is determined not as the result of what the candidate says or does, but is based on emotion.

It doesn't make a lot of sense to elect public officials on the basis of appearance and charm, but unfortunately this is the deciding factor in the minds of many voters.

Unexpected Happenings

You want to do things that your opponent isn't likely to do, like revealing his tax statement, or things your opponent would feel uncomfortable doing.

Spin

Don't be afraid to take the blame when things go wrong. On occasion they will.

We all have heard about "spin." And here is how to do it.

When you have a problem, admit it. By doing so you have established credibility.

Then use this credibility to define the problem in a way that keeps the political damage to a minimum.

The joy of this spin process lies in telling the accuser he is dead right and then getting the personal satisfaction of delineating what he or she is right about. It is important to admit your failings, not in order to gain ground on your opponent but to put the issue behind you. Having admitted your weakness and your opponent's strengths, the only things left to debate are *your strengths and your opponent's weaknesses.*

Building Up Your Opponent

Probably the nastiest trick you can pull on any competition is to build him or her up with expectations beyond his or her capabilities.

There have been primary elections for President where one of the candidates was way ahead in the polls and was expected to win by a landslide. When the results of the election were in, he won, but not by as wide a margin as the polls had indicated he would, so the media reported that he had, in effect, lost the election because he didn't live up to the expectations.

Lowballing/Sandbagging

In lowballing and sandbagging, the principle is the same: you want to create a handicapping system that makes any success of yours seem much bigger than it really is and your opponent's victory much smaller.

Truths About Dealing with People

People want to be sought after and talked to. I'll never forget the time I met with a businessman from our city who was higher than a kite, because the President had sent him a draft of a proposal and had asked him for his opinion.

Thoughts on How and Why People Vote the Way They Do

People want "Leadership," but there is much more. The voter feels he is incapable of figuring out what is going on. He is just interested in finding someone whom he feels somewhat comfortable with, who can handle the job, even if he or she disagrees with some of the things he or she advocates. If the voter believes the candidate can run it better than anyone else, he'll vote for him or her.

In the final analysis, candidates emphasize image over issues because they believe generally that most voters judge them on their personality rather than issues. People want to know what kind of person the candidate is. Is he or she likable? Of good character, honest, sincere, caring? Does he or she appear to be competent, that is, effective, knowledgeable and authoritative? It doesn't have anything to do with a candidate's ability to do the job, but people will be interested in family, and somewhere in your literature should be a picture of your family. That is, unless you are a mother with young children because, like it or not, there are still plenty of people who have a problem with a mother of young children out campaigning. I know it's not fair. But there are a lot of things in life that are not fair.

In many campaigns, successful candidates and many consultants feel that the decision on whom to vote for is based on emotion, not the positions of the candidate. We must like this person to vote for him or her. The issue in most elections is not, "Should we widen 30th Street?" or "Should we have term limits?" The real issue is the candidate.

Ideas

There is no substitute for a compelling idea. Some people believe that politics is a battle of ideas.

Old Time Political Advice

The average American doesn't want to be educated; he doesn't want to improve his mind; he doesn't even want to work consciously at being a good citizen.

But there are two ways you can interest him in a campaign and only two that have ever been found successful.

Most Americans love a contest. They like a good hot battle, with no punches pulled. So you can interest them if you put on a good fight! Also, most Americans like to be entertained. They like the movies, mysteries, fireworks and parades. So if you can't fight, put on a good show.

Three- and Five-Point Plans

I have been very successful in putting out and promoting three- and five-point plans during my campaigns. Nothing complicated. Just three or five things that I want to accomplish that the voters are familiar with and can relate to. As an example, in my first election as Mayor, I proposed things that I knew from my close contact with the citizens were of great interest—like redevelopment of our historic downtown area, bringing in new business to the city, etc.

These kinds of plans are easily understood and, if you win, you will be able to pull it out when you run for reelection and hopefully you will be able to say, as I was able to say, "What I said we would do, we did!"

Playbook

In football they use a playbook to which the players can refer. It is wise for the candidate or the campaign manager to also have a playbook. There are a million details and notes that you will want to write down for future reference. Being involved in a campaign is a learning process, and the information contained in your playbook will come in handy. When you finish the campaign, if you don't keep notes, you will often say to yourself such things as, "What the heck was that lady's name who was so knowledgeable about this or that?" or "Who was that committeewoman who had a friend who…?"

Don't scribble notes to yourself and throw them in a file. Keep a playbook. You can't carry the playbook around with you all the time so keep 3" x 5" cards in your pocket and jot down notes as you go along. Put them in an envelope glued inside your playbook.

Theme/Slogan/Core Message

Your campaign needs a theme/slogan/core message. You need to know the single most important message to be communicated to the voters. Develop a simple message after careful thought about who you are, what you are, what you stand for and what you plan to do. Then you need to repeat it over and over and over and over.

The purpose of the theme is to set you apart from all your opponents in the race. It is the answer to the voter's question, "Why should I support you?" The theme/slogan should capture the rationale for the campaign in a single, dramatic and persuasive way and should be a snappy phrase that can be easily recalled.

"Jimmy Jones, a good man doing a good job."
"Jimmy Jones, a big man doing a big job."
"Sarah Lopez gets things done at City Hall."
"Larry Smith is involved...he gets things done."
"I like Ike."
"Stephens, it's performance that counts."
"Linver, leadership for the '90s."

Two Main Factors Should Determine Your Campaign Theme

- ❖ *Policy issues that concern voters*
- ❖ *The personal characteristics and reputation of the candidate*

Jimmy Carter, when he was running for President, was positioned as a non-racist populist with farm boy honesty. He echoed his theme of "I'll never lie to you" over and over and over in speeches. The reporters loved it because it gave them a challenge. They looked for lies and found lots of them, but still Carter murmured, "Trust me, I'll never lie to you." He made trust his theme merely by claiming it.

Your slogan must be emphasized over and over and over throughout your campaign in speeches, bumper stickers, literature and all the rest of your advertising. By doing so, you will make it stick in the voter's mind.

Set the Agenda for the Campaign

You need to set the agenda, talk about yourself and what you plan to do and tell the world what your plans are. In my first campaign for Mayor, I said this again and again in person, in news releases, in literature.

"I've been deeply involved in this city for more than ten years, working with our citizens to make and keep Lenexa a great place to live and work, raise a family and do business. I have a record of accomplishment, involvement and pride in Lenexa. And I plan to continue on that course. I would appreciate your vote for Mayor."

It is important to contrast the candidate with the opponent in terms of style, experience, capabilities, values and alliances with interest groups. How the candidate is perceived is so important. This contrasting information makes an excellent format for a mailing piece.

Community Involvement

You need to be involved and visible in your community. Not just as a participant, but as a leader who has accomplished a lot.

Campaign Strategy and Tactics

There are many opportunities to be involved. And if you do a decent job, people notice.

The Five M's

A campaign is rolling along to victory when you are maximizing the five M's:

- ❖ Money
- ❖ Management
- ❖ Manpower (volunteers)
- ❖ Momentum
- ❖ Media

Correct Pronunciation

To some people this may seem like a very small thing, but to many people, including myself, correct pronunciation is very important. Nobody likes to have their name mispronounced or the name of their town mispronounced. I'm from a town called Lenexa. You hear all kinds of incorrect pronunciations. It's "Len-X-ah." I'm always annoyed when reporters on radio and television don't know how to pronounce a name or place. My wife is from Nevada, Missouri. It is pronounced "Na-vade-a," not "Na-vah-da." Or there is Miami, Oklahoma. In Florida it is pronounced "Mi-am-E," but the town in Oklahoma is pronounced "Mi-am-a."

And here in the Midwest those delicious nuts are called "pa-kahns," not "p-cans," and the pears are called "ahn-jew," not "ann-joe."

Opinion Leaders

You would do well to make sure the opinion leaders in your community know about your ideas. Stay in touch in person, via a letter, newsletter or fax. These people talk to many other people, and if they believe in you and your ideas, they can help you in your campaign. You don't know who the respected community leaders are? Here's how to find out and maybe get some good publicity at the same time. Send a survey to all the people you know who would be considered to be a community leader and ask them to anonymously list ten people who they feel are the true "community leaders." Tell them that you are taking an anonymous survey for the newspaper article you are writing. Thank them for taking the time to answer and include a stamped envelope addressed to you for the return. Not everybody will answer, but you will get a pretty good idea of who is well thought of. Take the information you have received and do write an article of a couple hundred words about who the community feels are their leaders. Call the paper and tell them about the survey. If the paper is on the ball at all, they will welcome the article with open arms.

And you will get some free publicity.

Leadership

There are many thoughts about leadership and many definitions of leadership. Some believe that it is simply getting people to the table and getting them to address the issues at hand.

I believe it includes the ability to get people of diverse opinions together and decide on a common course of action.

Political "Jujitsu"

It is important to find out what people perceive to be the biggest weakness of a candidate. Then use political "jujitsu" by advertising, highlighting, emphasizing, and otherwise stressing the very element of the campaign that the opponent is counting on to be your biggest weakness.

Problems and Solutions

In a campaign, if you bring up a problem, you are expected to have a solid, honest, real-world solution to that problem.

Answers to Questions

As part of your campaign, you need to sit down with your steering committee and draft answers, short and concise, for every possible question you think you will be asked during the campaign. This is generally not a long list because you will find that some basic questions will be asked repetitively. Why are you running? What do you feel are the main issues? How do you feel about XXXX?

While candidates should be prepared to respond to questions on a wide range of issues, they must have a single clear message that will convince voters. Then all the components of the campaign can be designed to advance that message. You're way ahead of the game if you take the time to do this. It is not that you are going to lie to a reporter, but you want to be sure you tell the person at this meeting the same answer you told the questioner at the meeting last night. Otherwise it sounds like you're "winging it" and flopping around like a mackerel. Be consistent.

Middle Class

You hear lots of discussion about the middle class in our society. Everybody has a different idea of who exactly should be classified that way. Regardless, in survey after survey, about 80 percent of Americans consider themselves to be a member of the middle class. Remember that as you plan your strategy.

Feminist Strategy/Minority Strategy

How often have you heard it said, "Vote for Betty because she's a woman" or "Vote for Jimmy because he's black"? I think we'll all be better off when candidates go into an election as professional, competent candidates and that we all elect the best candidate regardless of sex or race.

Shortcuts

There are no shortcuts. If you plan to run a quiet, well-mannered, bland campaign, it will be all but ignored by most of the electorate. If you want to be elected, make some noise, make some sparks fly, get your candidacy noticed.

Trust

Probably the most important relationship a campaigner must build with the voters is trust. If they don't trust you, they won't vote for you. If they do trust you, they will at least be willing to take a look.

A person is considered trustworthy when he or she is predictable, caring and faithful.

Homemakers for Linver, Teachers for Bowman, Etc.

You notice that I use the term homemaker and not "housewife." My wife hates that term. She also dislikes the expressions "little woman" or "the wife," and that is why I don't use them.

Anyway, often in a campaign you can get some extra mileage by organizing groups that have a particular reason to back the candidate. A group of homemakers that is interested in neighborhood improvements, a program that you are strongly backing, might be happy to form a group and go door to door handing out literature in your behalf. You could count on them to talk about you positively with friends at PTA meetings, while shopping, etc.

And a teachers' group might be willing to form a "Teachers for Dave Huff" campaign.

Third Candidates

A third candidate in a race for local or state office is often deliberately planted to pull the votes of ethnic and racial minorities from his opponent. It is designed to split the opponent's power base. It is based on the fact that, all things being equal, a given percentage of voters will vote for a name suggesting a religious, ethnic or racial affinity.

Non-political Elections

Who knows exactly how many elections are held each year? There are thousands of communities in the USA. And, in addition, every community has a host of civic clubs and organizations that select their leaders every year. Although this book is written primarily for people who are interested in being elected to and serving in the more than 500,000 elected public offices, many of the same principles can be used to be elected to a leadership position in your local organization.

Who's in Charge?

Only one person can be in charge of a campaign. And that person, after all is said and done, must be the candidate.

Know It All!

As a candidate, are you smart enough...and humble enough...to know what you *don't* know?

As I said before, a very smart political friend of mine told me a long time ago that you really don't start to find out what is going on until after you think you know it all.

Public Image

Someone once described public image as what the public sees, what the public knows and what the public believes about a candidate. A number of things go into making up this public image, including his or her performance record, personality, philosophy and competence. As a candidate, you believe certain things about yourself. Sure, you have to have self-confidence or you wouldn't be running in the first place. But what truly is your public image? It might do you well to have an independent source ask others in the community about their feelings about you. Ask the barber and the baker and the banker and the editor and the school principal and other public elected officials. The people who ask these questions need to be brutally honest when they report the answers back to you. You will find what I realized a long time ago, and that is not everybody thinks you are a wonderful human being. Now that is no reason to get down on yourself, because regardless of what you say or do, there will always—not sometimes—but always be people who will have a problem with you. Believe it!

Questions Asked of Female Candidates

A female candidate must still be prepared to answer such questions as, "Who's taking care of your kids while you're out campaigning?" and "Are you ever at home with your husband and family?" They wouldn't consider asking a man these same questions. I know it sounds crazy, but in the real world there are still those who don't understand the program and that women in public life are a fact of life and doing one terrific job.

City Council Races

In many communities candidates for City Council and Mayor run as individuals and not under a party banner. There are plenty of issues of concern in every city to make for interesting contests. Crime, street lighting, traffic, just to name a few.

Talking About the Big Issues

Not every minute of every day in a campaign is a Texas death match. In conversations with constituents or in a talk, you may make some light remarks about this or that and laugh a little, but you have to understand that when you need to get serious, you need to get serious very fast. That is true when you are discussing the "big" issues. They must be discussed seriously and without flippancy.

He or She Is One of Us

I'm sure you have heard a person say, "I'm voting for Joan Bowman because 'she's one of us.'" That is human nature. You have to belong. If you are new to a community, you need to get known and accepted before you can be "one of us." The quickest and best way to start is by joining a church, community clubs and organizations. You're better off to belong to three clubs and take an active leadership and helping role in them than to belong to 40 organizations and merely be listed as a member. People want to see you do good work, and they will praise you and remember you and support you when you decide to run for public office.

Your Car

If you are a candidate, you have to be smart enough not to run around campaigning in a Cadillac in a blue-collar neighborhood or in a Japanese car in an area where families live who work at General Motors.

Whipping Boy

Every candidate needs a whipping boy. That is, something or someone to be the target of the voters' wrath. Here are a few things that can be believed to be responsible for the current bad situation:

- ❖ The Legislature in the Capitol
- ❖ The people at City Hall
- ❖ The free-spending County Board

The Least Objectionable Candidate

Like it or not, many people don't like any of the candidates and either end up not voting or voting for the one whom they consider the least objectionable.

All Politics Is Local

Tip O'Neill, the former Speaker of the House, is credited with the expression, "All politics is local." He was probably correct, in that elections for the most part are decided on matters of local interest to the local voters. In these times, issues affecting the voter's pocketbook may be of greatest concern.

What's In It for Them?

People are interested in "What's in it for me?" not what you desire. Your approach needs to communicate to the recipient that you care about his or her needs and desires. It sets a positive tone, and the voter will react favorably toward what you have to say.

The Perfect Candidate

There are plenty of things to like and dislike about *all* candidates.

If you're looking for the "perfect" candidate, good luck. You're wasting your time. He or she doesn't exist.

Get Elected, Make a Difference!

Rich with Former Kansas Governor Mike Hayden

Chapter 7

Lists/Polls/Surveys

**The Best Advice from
Congresswoman Jan Meyers of Kansas**

> *"Listen to your constituents, and stay in touch with what they are thinking. Many issues will divide your constituency, and on a 50-50 issue you obviously can't please everyone. But those with whom you cannot vote should know you have listened, understood, and that you truly care about their interests and concerns."*

You may want to conduct surveys on your own—hire professionals if you are involved in a large election to do surveys on a contract basis. In every campaign you will have to deal with lists. Here are some of the lists that you will use:

❖ *VIP list of people for your area.* VIPs are people in your community who are activists or donors. They are PTA leaders, church leaders, business leaders, scout leaders, civic club leaders, homes association leaders, etc. These are people you need to be in contact with all the time for their views and concerns.

❖ *Media list.* The list of all the newspapers, radio stations, TV stations, cable TV outlets and community magazines serving your area. You need to know the correct spelling of the name of the reporter, the editor, the news director, the public service director, along with correct address, phone number and fax number.

❖ *Registered voter list.* This list which should have a record of a person's voting history is very valuable. They are available to candidates, so check with your county election office or Secretary of State. You will notice that many people vote only in certain types of elections. Some vote only in school elections. Some vote only in primary elections. Some vote only in general elections. Some vote only in Presidential elections. Some people vote in each and every single election.

❖ *Supporter list.* This list has the names, addresses and phone numbers of anybody who has indicated to you that they are a friend of yours who would support you or who you feel would support you.

❖ *Potential contributor list.* This list is anyone who has contributed to your opponent, as well as anyone who has supported or contributed to previous candidates for the office you are seeking. (Check with your Secretary of State or local election office as to where past financial records are kept. These records are open to the public.) It should also contain the names of community leaders like bankers and other businessmen and women to whom good government means good business. It will contain the names of those who might or should contribute to your campaign for whatever reason.

- ❖ *Membership lists* for various clubs and organizations, professional associations, religious organizations, etc. These are very useful for mailings emphasizing why they should support you. Ask the members of your steering committee for a list of the movers and shakers in the community. They are the ones who belong to all kinds of organizations.

- ❖ *Absentee voter list* and potential absentee voter list. The rules regarding absentee voting are being relaxed in many states. Check with your local election office for the current rules. This list contains some people living in nursing homes, business people who travel a lot, military people who keep their home community as their legal address, and college students, etc.

Polling and surveys to find out what the voters are thinking and what the issues are continue to be used in more and more campaigns of all sizes. There is quality information, but there's also nonsense and misinformation that comes about as the result of polls and surveys. For purposes of this book, I will use the terms polling and surveys as though they were the same thing. There is a technical difference, but for a candidate for a local or state office it is insignificant. Technically, polls result from probability sample surveys where a statistically accurate group of people is questioned. Whereas a survey is really nothing more than asking people questions and marking down their answers. It is not necessarily statistically correct.

Some polls are probably very accurate, but many are designed to agree with a preconceived result and conclusion. There are many people who play games with surveys. If you are willing to bet the farm on them, you probably also believe in the tooth fairy.

Surveys Are Used in Campaigns to:

- Discover the issues and formulate strategy.
- Determine the name ID (name recognition of the candidate).
- Pump up the enthusiasm of the volunteers when you have a good survey.
- Raise money for a campaign. Contributors like to see that their money is going to go to a winner. A good survey can bring in big dollars.
- Get publicity for the campaign and for the candidate himself or herself. A good survey is news. (So is a bad one, so be sure you keep those quiet and away from the news media.)

Conducting Surveys

Even small races can afford some type of survey. I don't want you to get the idea that all of them are no good. I just want you to keep your eyes open and understand that there are plenty of people out there who play games with surveys. And there are politicians who believe in "finger-in-the-wind" politics. With each new survey and each new issue they change positions.

As a candidate using a good survey, you may very well find out that issues you thought were really important to the voter were of little interest to them and vice versa.

Some of the Factors that Determine the Validity of a Survey Are:

- *The questions that are being asked.* Are they well thought out and clear? If ten people hear the question, will they all understand it to mean the same thing?
- *Who is doing the interviewing?* If the person being interviewed knows that the person doing the interviewing is working on behalf of candidate "X," then you can be sure that he will be complimentary to candidate "X."
- *Who is being surveyed?* Have the people been randomly selected from the specific group you want to interview?

These are the main considerations, but there are many others. In a small campaign you might want to contact the political science department at your local college for assistance in putting together and conducting a survey. In larger campaigns there are all kinds of professionals who will work with you for a fee. Like anything else, some are better than others. Be sure to get references and check with the candidates whom they have worked with in the past.

Straw Polls

Early in an election one candidate or another will dominate a gathering in his area, neighborhood or home town. Then he or she will proceed to stack the deck, like buying the most tickets to a fund-raiser and passing them out to supporters. Each ticket can be used as one vote in a "straw poll"! At the event each person with a ticket writes the name of the person whom they favor on the back and drops it into a big box. The tickets are counted by a blue ribbon group at the event, and the results are announced with plenty of fanfare, and with follow-up in the press. I got myself a real education the first couple of times I was involved in this scam as a candidate who couldn't afford to buy a huge amount of tickets to stack the deck and win the straw poll. Thus, I didn't get the publicity as the leading candidate.

Computers

This book is not going to teach you how to use or program your computer, but they can make your campaign very efficient and accurate, and you won't be flying by the seat of your pants the way many campaigns were conducted in the past. It is now easy to update and correct information on a P.C.

There are computer services that can also be of great help to you. But if you want to keep your campaign information confidential, try to find a friend who is a computer whiz and even better if he or she has some political wherewithal. The ideal person is one who has had some political experience and knows how to get the most out of computer data.

Chapter 8

Budget

**The Best Advice from
U.S. Senator Paul Simon of Illinois**

"Work hard; stand for what you believe, rather than what the polls may suggest; and try to help people who otherwise might not be helped. The rich and powerful can take care of themselves pretty well. But many struggling Americans need a helping hand and an opportunity."

Get Money...Establish Your Budget/War Chest

Drawing up a budget is tricky business. Obviously, a statewide race will be more expensive than a race for a City Council seat. As good a guide as anything is to see what the last candidate for the office you are seeking spent and add 20 percent to it. I suggest you set up a "bare bones" budget. If you get more contributions than you have budgeted for, you can make an executive decision as to how to spend those funds most efficiently in your election effort.

Here are the major expense considerations in setting a budget. (The size and scope of your campaign will determine what applies.)

- Headquarters rent and utilities
- Staff (if you have any paid professionals)
- Consultant fees
- Equipment rental like copier, fax, computer (try to borrow these)
- Cost of phones for office for "Get Out the Vote" effort and polling
- Cost of cellular phone and pager rental
- Cost of stationery
- Postage for mailings and postal permits
- Newspaper, radio and TV advertising
- Billboard advertising
- Direct mail advertising
- Yard signs and stakes
- Bus cards if you live in a metro area with lots of bus traffic
- Bumper stickers, lapel stickers, buttons
- Door hangers
- All kinds of advertising specialties from fingernail files to combs to coffee mugs to key rings to T-shirts to balloons
- Cost of good photos of you for the literature

- ❖ Printing
- ❖ Special events like a rally, an open house, a reception
- ❖ Travel, meals and hotel/motel
- ❖ Cost of polling and surveys
- ❖ Design and preparation of brochures and literature for handouts, mailings, invitations
- ❖ Cost of lists of voters
- ❖ Cost of family labels. Family labels are labels that are addressed to the "XXXX Family," rather than each person who is an eligible voter receiving a separate piece of mail. Individual mailing can get to be tremendously expensive, and I don't think it is worth the extra cost.
- ❖ Cost of election day activities like special mailings, transportation and victory party (you should be able to get a friend or a group of friends to pay for the victory party).

In any campaign, 60 to 80 percent of the budget should go to advertising! That includes direct mail, radio, TV, newspapers, publicity, news releases, handouts, bumper stickers, yard signs, etc.

Note: Radio stations, TV stations and most newspapers and printers expect to be paid cash. Some vendors will extend credit, but they still expect to get paid, whether you win or lose the election. A while back when I was in a campaign for Governor, I limited myself to no more than $10,000 in debt at any time. I had so many offers of credit it would have been easy to go up to hundreds of thousands of dollars in debt real fast. Many a candidate has gone overboard only to lose the election and find himself or herself in debt for years afterward. Be *very* careful regarding debt.

You need to decide the absolute limit of your own personal financial involvement with the campaign. What are you willing to spend and what is this adventure worth to you? You need to be prepared to loan some seed money to the campaign to get things started. But you need to know that you may not get your money back. Many a candidate in the heat of the battle has done all kinds of things that he or she regretted later, like taking out huge loans or mortgaging their home. Those are hard decisions to make, but don't make them lightly. If you win, you will probably be able to recoup your investment. If you lose, in most cases, you can kiss that money good-bye.

In the heat of a campaign, all kinds of ideas come forth, and they all cost money. Don't let yourself get carried away. You have a budget and a plan. Take your time and think about it and, as my mother used to say, sleep on the idea before you deviate from your budget plan. Act in haste, and repent at leisure.

Campaign Treasurer

Your campaign treasurer is **not** a fund-raiser. This person makes sure that you have money in the till to pay the bills as they come due and control cash flow. He or she holds the reins on spending. He or she should be realistically tightfisted to manage the money flow in the campaign. The treasurer has the responsibility of making sure that all contributions and expenses are recorded and reported in accordance with state law as they come due. It is a good idea to photocopy each and every check you receive.

Periodically throughout the campaign you will probably need to file campaign finance reports (check with your Secretary of State). Put controls on spending. Decide in advance who will give the okay to authorize any spending. Should it be the treasurer, the campaign manager, or the candidate, or all three? Should all checks have at least two signatures?

Don't spend or authorize to spend money that you cannot reasonably expect to have in cash—real soon. Don't rely on pledges or promises. Nothing beats greenbacks.

Seed Money

When you open your campaign account at the local bank, you may have to loan some of your own money to the campaign as seed money to get the account started. Find a friendly banker and he or she will counsel you as to the best type of account at that bank to have for a campaign. You will need to write checks. Who will sign them? Will the bank charge you a service charge? If so, how much?

Planning When to Spend Advertising Dollars

Always work backward from election day. How far back you work depends on how much money you have. A large percentage of voters is influenced to vote or reminded to vote at the last minute, and many of them do not make up their minds until they walk into the voting booth. It is important that you get that name recognition registered in their minds just before the election so it sticks in their minds (positively) as they vote.

Get Elected, Make a Difference!

Rich with Missouri Governor Mel Carnahan

Chapter 9

Fund-raising

**The Best Advice from
Congresswoman Karen McCarthy of Missouri**

> "Perhaps the most valuable advice I can pass on to someone wanting to become involved in public service is to pay attention to detail and be sure to follow up on whatever you tell someone you will do. In today's political climate, people are often cynical. Every problem you solve, every letter you respond to, every phone call you return tells an individual they are important to you and helps to establish a good working relationship."

As the name implies, you are soliciting funds from any and all sources, by means of direct mail, telephone or in person.

In planning for a campaign, asking, "How much money will we need?" is sort of like asking, "How long is a piece of string?" It all depends!

When it comes to fund-raising, you'll be amazed at how many experts you have out there among your friends who know just how to do it and who should give how much. But you will find that many are unwilling to even ask their friends for money. Finding individuals who will actually ask another individual in person for money is as difficult as pulling teeth from a chicken.

May the Lord bless the soul of the one person on your steering committee, your fund-raising chairman or chairwoman, who has the overall responsibility for fund-raising and does a good job of it. In some campaigns that person is called the finance chairman, but I think it is best to describe the actual charge that the person has, and that is to raise funds for the campaign. I call that person the fund-raising chairman or chairwoman. The truth of the matter is that the candidate also needs to be deeply involved and must ask for donations from those capable of giving larger contributions.

You have to solicit large contributions in person. In person, or through the mail, always ask for a specific amount. You should have a pretty good idea of what you expect from that person. Don't just ask for a contribution. If you do, you'll find that you will receive $10 contributions from people who should give you $100.

Your fund-raising efforts must be coordinated with other members of the steering committee. You'll ask people for money in person, over the phone, through the mail at fund-raisers, coffees, dinners, etc. The fund-raising chairperson will be working with many other volunteers involved in the campaign.

Legally Collecting Campaign Contributions

The fund-raising chairperson and your legal advisor should confer before you attempt to raise funds so everybody knows what the current rules are regarding campaign finance. There are all kinds of state and local regulations, and your Secretary of State's office should be contacted about this and about the dates that campaign finance reports are due from all candidates.

Whose money will you accept and whose money will you not accept? I have always operated on the philosophy that I'll accept anybody's money as long as it is green. When you give me money for a campaign, you know that all you are doing is buying good government. I know that is contrary to the thinking of many people who are very careful from whom they accept money. This is a call for the candidate to make. I have never had a problem with the way I operate. I look at it this way. I need money to operate a campaign, and if a person wants to give me money and understands that all he or she will get for that money is access to me or for a chance to get in his or her side of the story, that is okay with me. I listen to everybody anyway. I always have—even those who haven't given me money.

In 1995, Senator Dole made a speech in Hollywood condemning the entertainment industry, especially Time-Warner, for some of the product that it puts out on the market. When it was discovered that Time-Warner had donated $21,000 to Dole over the years, Dole said something to the effect, "See, they didn't buy me."

Thank You

It goes without saying that you need to thank all your contributors, by mail, and in person when you see them. The fund-raising committee volunteers should prepare thank you letters for the candidate to sign. In smaller campaigns, the candidate can scribble out personal notes.

Fund-raising Methods

Besides the candidate or the fund-raising chairperson asking people for money in person, you can have all kinds of events for that purpose. Over the years many methods have been used to get funds for a campaign. The traditional methods are eye-to-eye, over the phone, by direct mail solicitation, dinners, lunches, breakfasts, receptions, coffees and picnics. My supporters have put on silent auctions of merchandise as part of the reception, and it has been very successful in bringing in substantial amounts of money. Have some friends and supporters sponsor one of these events. They merely find a location, invite potential contributors, and take care of all the details to ensure that it is a success. It is their event to be as creative as they wish. These methods work.

Note: The idea is to put on as big a deal as possible, spending as little as possible, to raise the maximum number of dollars for the campaign.

There are many other ways. Candidates have been known to put ads in the newspaper asking for money or distributing flyers door to door asking for money. Or selling campaign material like hats, buttons, T-shirts, etc. Before you try these methods, I suggest you try the traditional methods. They all take work, but *the idea is to raise the most money with the least effort.*

Professional Fund-raisers/Telemarketing for Funds

Yes, there are professional fund-raisers available who will raise money for your campaign for a fee. Some are very good, some are so-so and some are sleazy. Many a candidate has found out the hard way that when you turn over the job of raising funds to an "outsider," you have problems. While some of these organizations do very good work, in most cases they don't do anything that you couldn't just do yourself. Even if you hire one of these companies, they will still want you deeply involved to help them make contact with the best prospects.

Telemarketing is being used more and more for political fund-raising. There is no doubt that you can raise considerable sums. You have to pay a very hefty commission for all the funds they raise. But, as I have said before, whenever there's an outsider raising funds, I get a little nervous. I'd be extremely concerned what the solicitor is saying to the prospective donor.

If this method of fund-raising appeals to you, I would suggest that you mail to all your prospects *first*, telling them about yourself, your programs and asking them for a specific amount of money. You should be able to rake the cream off the top, and you will know that your prospects will have some ideas about you and your programs before they get the pitch over the phone from a telemarketing person. You could then be satisfied that they truly earned their commissions on any money they raised.

The biggest downside to having an outsider doing the fund-raising, as far as I am concerned, is that you don't know what they are telling the prospective donor in extracting the money from them. You really won't know until maybe long after they have left town.

If you insist on hiring a fund-raiser, you should personally make a lot of phone calls and contacts with past candidates for whom they have worked. I'd even go so far as to check the finance reports of the candidate, find out who contributed, and then contact some of the contributors. Do I sound suspicious? You bet I do.

Tips for Your Direct Mail Fund-raising Letter

In composing your fund-raising letter, ask yourself, "What would I want to know about a candidate if he or she asked me for money?"

Then:

- ❖ Make it as personal as you can.
- ❖ Write plainly; don't get too formal.
- ❖ Start the letter with a "grabber" phrase or comment to get their attention.
- ❖ In a sentence or two tell why you are running, what the main issue is, how it affects the person receiving the letter and what you plan to do about it.
- ❖ Be enthusiastic and talk like a winner. People want to give to campaigns that they feel have a fighting chance of winning.

- The more emotional the appeal, the more money it will produce.
- Don't get too windy! Get to the point, "Send money!" You are expected to say that; don't beat around the bush.
- Direct mail experts claim the best months for soliciting funds are October, April and March, in that order.
- The left side of your campaign stationery should list the many community leaders, your steering committee, the people who are with you in this campaign.
- Ask for a specific amount. Don't dillydally around. "Your check for $100 will be used for advertising the last week of the campaign, but I need it now to reserve the space." It is critical that you create a sense of urgency in your letter.
- Ask them to make their checks out to "Schwartz for Council committee."
- Give them a great big Thank You in advance for their support.
- Personally sign the letter.
- Always, not sometimes or occasionally, but always add a one line P.S. in your own writing in which you ask them a second time for money. Many people read the P.S. of a letter before they read the letter. Everyone knows that if you get a letter from a candidate, it will ask for money. So go ahead and ask for money.
- Include a business reply envelope with your letter so the recipient can just write a check and mail it back to you without having to look for an envelope and a

stamp. You want to make it as easy as you can for a person to give.

Direct mail is the darling of fund-raising for generating a large number of smaller contributions. It is a great way to broaden your base of support.

When to Start Raising Funds?

The best answer is as soon as possible. There are campaign laws that differ from state to state regarding when you can start. Check with your Secretary of State.

A Contributor's Investment in You

Once a person has put their money on the line for you, whether it be $1 or $500, they are committed to you. Sure there are companies and some individuals who like to hedge their bets and work both sides of the street. They donate to both—or all—candidates. But generally a contributor, after giving you money, will sing your praises to their friends. In effect, anybody who gives you $10 is a walking billboard for you.

In-kind Contributions

Not everyone is willing to give you cash. You will be offered all kinds of things in-kind rather than cash—like supplies, food, meeting rooms at the hotel for a reception, stakes for yard signs, printing, etc. If it is something that you would have to pay cash for anyway, take it. Remember that you have to report in-kind contributions just as you report cash contributions.

PACs (Political Action Committees)

PACs are put together to raise money for causes that they wish to promote. Company employees form PACs, as do Realtors, bankers, auto workers, doctors, etc. Their members contribute and then decide amongst themselves who they will support and how much they will contribute to a particular candidate.

There are thousands of PACs. Some local and state PACs will possibly contribute to your campaign. Most of the larger PACs are located in Washington and support congressional candidates.

Some candidates, as a matter of policy, will not accept any money from PACs. They feel as though you are obligating yourself to the program of the PAC from whom you received the money. But is that any different than accepting money from the ladies who are lobbying to have a stop sign put up on their corner? Isn't this just a matter of degree? Sure, it is a matter of degree, but if you can be "bought" for a contribution, you're not fit to be a candidate anyway. You should have higher standards than that.

My friend, Paul Ingam, with whom I served on the City Council years ago, always jokingly says to me whenever we reminisce about those days, "Hey, if it weren't for the graft, you could hardly have made ends meet." Then we have a big belly laugh and talk about what a great experience it was for both of us and still is for me to serve in public office.

Fund-raising Invitation Follow-up

It is in your best interest to have a volunteer committee call the people to whom you sent invitations to your big-deal, big-dollar fund-raiser. "Hello, this is Jimmy Long at the Joan Bowman for Mayor campaign headquarters. Did you receive the invitation to the lunch for Joan on Thursday, February 17th?" You may have to prod some people into coming, or at least sending in their money, whether they show up or not. It is not unheard of for a candidate to find out who has sent in their money, and will not be able to make it. They then resell the table at a sold-out event a second time to somebody else.

You have heard me say this before, but book your event in a room where you barely have enough room and people have to stand in the halls, or you have to put overflow tables in the hallway. Nothing is more impressive and will get people talking than standing room only. And nothing is more depressing to the attendees than to be in a small group in a huge room. That can make your campaign event look like a loser.

R.S.V.P. to Invitations

Regardless of whether it is a big-deal dinner or a private get-together, always ask for an R.S.V.P. Regardless, you will find that only about half the people, if that many, will reply one way or the other.

The Pitch

At the dinner, have fun and enjoy. Invite a well-known person to be the speaker. And be sure the talk is not too long and windy. Thank those in attendance for their sponsorship of the event and for being there.

At a private get-together, take a couple of minutes and have the host or hostess introduce you for some short, informal comments. The candidate should thank the host and hostess and the attendees for being there. Then you make your pitch for their money. Sometimes several guests offer "spontaneous" prearranged pledges out loud. That sometimes get the others involved and fired up. Emphasize that you sincerely appreciate them for being here and being willing to put their money where their mouth is.

Hitting Them Again for Funds

If a person has contributed to you once, there is a pretty good chance they will contribute a second, even a third time. Experts in the direct mail area know that and use it effectively all the time. In your campaign you will have a time when you desperately need funds for something. That is a good time to send a letter to your contributors and pitch your need.

Your Fund-raising Letter Does Double Duty

In any fund-raising letter, you are asking for money. But never forget that it is also the vehicle you can use to tell more good things about your candidacy. Even if the recipient doesn't send you money, you are selling yourself, selling your ideas, selling your philosophy. And hopefully helping to convince him or her to vote for you.

A Membership Club

It is not unusual for an elected official or even a candidate to ask people to join his or her "club." As an example, you could have a Legislator's "breakfast club." These clubs usually cost members anywhere from $50 on up to join. Members receive some sort of recognition as a member of the club and have the privilege of paying for their own breakfast when the group gets together. The legislator in this scenario would bring the members up to date on what is happening regarding legislation, or a candidate can talk about the campaign and the issues. He or she may even bring another elected official as a guest and introduce him or her around. The money to join the club goes into the campaign fund of the candidate or the legislator's campaign fund to pay for unreimbursed expenses of running for and being in office, and carrying out the duties of the office.

People like to belong. And people, especially businessmen and women, want to be sure they stay close to their legislator so they can get their side of the issue heard. This is a form of insurance.

Peer Fund-raising

If you have a doctor or a lawyer or a teacher on your steering committee, ask him or her to send a letter to his or her peers in support of you asking for money. It works. It is a good method of raising funds.

It Helps Fund-raising When a Devil Is Present

Fund-raising guru Richard Viguerie said the secret of success in direct mail fund-raising is that "for a crusade to succeed, there must be a devil present. When one isn't present, one must be created. You need to remember that recipients are more likely to respond out of fear and negativism than they are to *support* a campaign or cause from an emotionally positive point of view. The hard, if unappealing, fact is: most people will do far more to hurt their enemies than they will do to help their friends."

Senator Bob Dole and Rich

Chapter 10

Direct Mail/Mailings/Literature

▼

The Best Advice from
U.S. Senator Rick Santorum of Pennsylvania

"Here are nine points that I believe to be crucial to any campaign for public office:

1. Analyze your opponent and the voters.

2. Include your family in your decision to run.

3. Believe in yourself and be confident in your ability to win.

4. Put a plan together on how you are going to win.

5. Work harder than you ever have.

6. Study the issues.

7. Know why you want to win and articulate it with passion.

8. Stick to your plan.

9. Carve out time for your family every week and don't waver."

Literature Preparation

All literature, posters, bumper stickers, buttons, etc. should have the same advertising theme, the same basic design and typestyles and the same colors. Make sure the type on literature is large enough so it can be read easily by senior citizens. Leave plenty of white space. Make the message simple and clear. I have very effectively used lots of pictures with captions in large print.

Also in the preparation of literature and direct mail pieces, make sure they do not contain any typos or mistakes. Often these pieces are proofread it seems hundreds of times—and mistakes still occur. Before it goes to press, pass around the final draft to be proofread by a number of people.

Thoughts on Direct Mail

The key is to make your mailings effective from a standpoint of how they look and what they say.

Good direct mail letters to voters are always written from one person to another and filled with dozens of "you's" and "I's."

The opening paragraph is usually some sort of urgent, important message about how your lifestyle or something near and dear to you is being threatened. The rest of the letter tells why it is important for the candidate to get elected so he or she can get rid of this nasty enemy, and that would greatly benefit the recipient.

Political direct mail letters should be emotional, not dry and dull. Talk about anger and fear. Identify the enemy in human terms: "the welfare chiseler," "his hand in my pocket," etc. Ask

Direct Mail/Mailings/Literature

for their advice. Ask them for a favor. Ask for a very specific dollar amount to be used for a specific purpose—postage to send mailing to voters about the "truth" about this or that to combat the misinformation (lies) being put out by the opponent, or to buy radio ads the week before the election, etc.

All your mail is important, but some is more important than others. I know it gets expensive, but use first class if it is absolutely important that the recipient receive your letter. Also, if the addressee has moved, the letter will be returned to you if it is undeliverable. With bulk mail, the mail is *not* returned to you. The quality of mail service is spotty around the country. Locally, I've had no problems over the years, but I have had bulk mail sent to post offices outstate for delivery that took a month to get delivered. I suggest you check with other candidates about their recent experiences with mailings. Frankly, there are too many people who consider bulk mail to be junk mail, and treat it as such. And a piece of campaign literature delivered *after* election day is of no value.

By targeting direct mail—sending to a select group of people—you can save postage and reach those who are your most likely prospects. As an example, in primary elections, usually only a small percentage of registered voters actually vote. Some candidates will go through voter lists and only mail to those people who show a history of voting in primary elections, thus saving postage. Sometimes candidates from the same party who are not running against each other will share mailings. That is, they will both insert their literature in the same envelope and mail, and split the postage. Or they will have one flyer printed with both names on it, and mail, thus sharing both printing and mailing costs.

Direct mail professionals say that November is always the best month to solicit funds through the mail, followed by September and October. The summer months are usually the pits.

Your letters, whether soliciting funds or talking about the campaign, should be personally signed.

Every letter, every piece of literature, regardless of what its main purpose is, should somewhere include the campaign theme, "sell the candidate," and ask for money. Everything you send is a form of advertising.

With a computer and a computer maven on your steering committee, you will be able to do a lot of personalization of letters without a great amount of hassle. You can send targeted letters to specific groups like veterans, lawyers, teachers, etc.

A technique that is effective is to find a lawyer friend to send a letter on his or her own stationery to his or her fellow lawyers asking for money in your behalf. The same goes for teachers, accountants, bankers, etc.

Besides personal letters, there are all kinds of mailing formats that can be purchased from direct mail houses. The letter that looks similar to a telegram format is only one of many available.

Always, not sometimes or occasionally, add a P.S. at the bottom of **all** your campaign letters. It is not uncommon to even have a P.P.S.

When it comes to fund-raising, remember that the only thing most people want back for their money is good government. And sure, some people do give because it is in their best interests.

For some reason, which nobody seems to have an answer for, fund-raising letters which are signed in blue ink have a greater dollar return than letters signed in black ink.

If your campaign will be mailing several times to the voters, you should consider a mailing using postcards. Before you mail or print, check with the post office for the rates. I have used oversized postcards, regular-sized postcards, and 8-1/2" x 11" cards printed on both sides. I'm a great believer in two-sided flyers and cards with your name in big bold letters on both sides.

An Important Note About Lists

All lists are always in a state of flux. They are constantly changing. People are moving, getting married, getting divorced, joining organizations, quitting organizations, etc. Many times the lists contain inaccurate information in the first place with wrong addresses or misspelled names. A direct mail expert I know told me that it is not at all unusual to find that more than 20 percent of a list that has been mailed to will be returned because they are deceased or have moved.

In my race for Governor, I mailed to the list of past contributors to the previous Governor candidate. They were mailed first class, and I was shocked to find that more than 25 percent of the letters were returned by the post office.

Computer/Data Processing

You'll need an experienced, talented, creative computer person deeply involved in the campaign. Computers can do wonderful things if you have a person who really knows how to operate them. Here are just a few of the things you can store in your computer, pull out, or move around at will, edit and change: media lists, contributor lists, information for campaign finance reports, voter lists, voting patterns, your speeches, correspondence, personalized letters, thank you notes, issues information, mailing labels, address information, phone numbers, locations for yard signs, etc., etc. Much of the time-consuming handwritten work of past elections has been replaced by computer programs. You can get a compact disc (a CD) that contains voter information on every registered voter in your state. Record keeping is so much easier these days.

When you write copy for a letter, postcard, flyer, any campaign material, always be upbeat and positive about the campaign and the candidate. Never, never be defensive.

Your final mailing before the election (to arrive the day before the election), preferably an oversized card or a flyer, should list the voter's polling place. This is important because polling places in some areas do change frequently. And new voters may not be familiar with where they vote. Yes, I understand that notices of changes are sent out by the election commissioner, but most people probably threw them away.

With any bulk rate mailings you do, check with the post office regarding carrier route sorting. You will save some money.

A Few Thoughts About Postage and Mailings

Postage will eat you up alive if you don't keep an eye on it and make sure your mailings are efficient and effective.

On mailings, it is best to use actual postage stamps rather than a printed bulk mail indicia or a meter mail stamp. A hand-addressed letter or postcard is better than one addressed using a stick-on label. Some people claim that commemorative stamps on envelopes get a better response than regular stamps.

Direct Mail/Mailings/Literature

Bulk mailings, third class mailings, need to be prepared for mailing in very precise fashion according to postal regulations. Frankly they are a pain and considered by many to be junk mail and quickly discarded by the recipient. (I always put my name in big bold letters on both sides of any piece of bulk mail, so that even if a person pitches it the moment he or she receives it, they can't miss seeing my name on the way to the wastebasket.)

Many times in fund-raising appeals, it helps to get a business reply permit from the post office. When you send the prospective contributor your solicitation letter, you include a business reply envelope. You set up a fund at the post office, and for each of these envelopes you receive back, you pay the post office for the postage and a fee depending on how many you expect back. This is effective, because people can pull out their checkbooks on the spot, write a check, put it in an envelope and mail it without having to find an envelope, rewrite your address or find a stamp.

You need to be aware that you will receive a number of these envelopes back with nasty notes or just empty, or filled with Bible tracts or off-the-wall literature. I've gotten many of them.

Literature/Yard Sign Distribution

Door-to-door distribution of literature and the putting up of yard signs requires a person who can organize crews of two or three people who can go out and work together in particular areas. The lists of yard sign locations are collected as the campaign progresses from supporters, from names collected by the people doing the phoning who are in your camp, and from people who say okay as you campaign door to door. The signs are usually most effective if they are all put up on the weekend about ten days prior to the election. Different communities have different laws regulating yard signs. Check with your city hall.

For literature distribution in some campaigns, it is effective to gather a group of supporters the weekend before the election, and all get together at a central location like the headquarters for a cup of coffee and doughnuts before heading out. It creates an atmosphere of friendship, and you should have it mapped out as to who covers what streets, etc.

There is nothing wrong with handing out some literature at headquarters to individuals who "will pass it out for you." But be very careful, because oftentimes the material ends up in the trunk of the person's car and is never used. The same is true of yard signs and bumper stickers. Just because a person stops by headquarters and asks for a bumper sticker and a button, don't get the idea that he or she is going to proudly wear the button and put the bumper sticker on the back of their car. Very often these people are collectors who don't have anything better to do, so they are making the rounds of all the campaign offices collecting stickers, buttons and other handout material you have to give away.

Chapter 11

Research

The Best Advice from
Congressman Bill Emerson of Missouri

"Always listen to what the folks have to say and always stay in touch with your constituency so you can reflect their views in the governmental process.

Listening is an attribute that many politicians have a tough time capturing. Many think that they have to push or press their ideas for the future by always talking. I have found that simply by listening carefully and thoroughly to similar or opposite points of view from my own that folks better appreciate what I am trying to accomplish for them in Congress. If a person is approachable, they gain the public's trust. Listening is a first step in that process.

For anyone currently in or seeking public office, it is vitally important to know what's on the minds of the people you want to serve. This is accomplished by staying in touch, and I try to do this various ways. When I have to be in Washington for Congressional business, my district staff is very attentive to the pulse of my constituency, while I keep in touch by reading the mail and listening to messages left by telephone. Then I follow up to each person who contacts me with a personal letter. It is a two-way street—I find out what is on their minds, and then through a postal response, they find out I have heard from them.

Another point I do not want to overlook is the best way to stay in touch is by meeting with folks. I make every opportunity during weekends and Congressional recesses to return home to listen and get a hands-on sense of what's important to my constituency in southern Missouri."

Do the in-depth research necessary on past elections, the opposition candidate, the issues, information on position papers on various subjects, census data, voting patterns, etc. Make sure the information contained in the campaign literature and in candidate speeches is accurate.

In every political campaign, regardless of size, you need:

- ❖ **Voter Research** of past elections and voting habits to determine who are most likely to vote for you, and who you most likely need to convince to vote for you to win.
- ❖ **Issue Research** to determine what issues will be important in the election, but be sure you have the facts.
- ❖ **Opposition Research** to determine your opponent's background and voting record, etc.

Voter Research

In every voting area you need to accurately know the results of the past several elections for the office you are seeking. If it was a partisan race, you need to know the vote totals by party affiliation. You need to know the total number of registered voters by party, by age, by sex, what recent elections they have voted in, as well as ethnic background if available.

There will be common concerns among all the voters, and many neighborhoods will have their own specific concerns that you must address. It won't take you long to determine that there are many things that would be great to do, but you will not be able to because of the constraints of time, limited number of volunteers and limited funds. So you have to make some hard decisions.

You will need to focus on those voters who are necessary to get you elected. You have to understand that not every voter is going to vote for you. You will focus on the voters of your party, the person who votes in every election, the person who supports your positions on issues or is likely to support those positions, etc. You should **not** spend a great deal of time trying to get people to register to vote. Everybody has an excuse, but if they were really interested, they should have registered a long time ago on their own. Also, you should **not** try to educate the voters on all the facets of each and every issue. That is not what they expect from you.

"Historical" Voters

The voter who votes in almost all elections and has over a period of years is called an "historical" voter. They are precious, and you need to court them. Rain or shine, for whatever reason, you can count on them voting. And, hopefully, for you. You absolutely must reach those historical voters.

Targeting

Willie Sutton, the infamous bank robber, was asked why he robbed banks, and he said, "Because that's where the money is." In that same vein, as a politician, you need to search for votes and name recognition where the votes are.

You need to "target" the voters who are most likely to vote for you. (These scenarios are designed to give you an idea of how to do targeting. It is not intended to be an absolute guide regarding primary elections, general elections, runoff elections or special elections, etc., because the laws regarding specifically who can vote in what elections varies considerably from state to state. For the specific regulations in your state, contact your Secretary of State.)

Situation #1 *(A nonpartisan primary election for Mayor in a medium-sized community)*

You need to know:

- ❖ XXXX adults live in area.
- ❖ There are XXXX registered voters.

❖ XXXX people actually voted in the last *primary* election.

In a *nonpartisan primary election* you need to target all the people who voted in the last election, as well as any eligible voter who has registered since the last election.

Situation #2 *(A partisan primary election for State Representative in a medium-sized community)*

You need to know:

❖ XXXX adults live in area.

❖ XXXX are registered Democrats.

❖ XXXX are registered Republicans.

❖ XXXX are registered as unaffiliated.

❖ XXXX people actually voted in the last *primary election*. Of those:

❖ XXXX were Democrats.

❖ XXXX were Republicans.

❖ XXXX were unaffiliated. (People who are registered as unaffiliated/Independent are not allowed to vote in partisan primary elections in some states, but this will vary from state to state)

In this election, as a candidate, you need to target all the eligible voters (check with your Secretary of State) who voted in the last *primary* election, as well as any eligible voter who has registered since then.

Situation #3 *(A nonpartisan primary election for Mayor in the general election)*

You need to know:

- XXXX adults live in area.
- There are XXXX registered voters.
- XXXX people actually voted in the last *primary* election.

As a candidate, you need to target **all** the people who voted in the last *general* election, as well as any voter who has registered since then.

Situation #4 *(A partisan general election for State Senator in a medium-sized area)*

You need to know:

- XXXX adults live in area.
- There are XXXX registered voters.
- XXXX are registered Democrats.
- XXXX are registered Republicans.
- XXXX are registered unaffiliated.

- ❖ XXXX people actually voted in the last general election. Of those:
- ❖ XXXX were Democrats.
- ❖ XXXX were Republicans.
- ❖ XXXX were unaffiliated.

All voters can potentially vote for you in this election. But in this election, as an example, if you are a Democrat, you will target the Democrats who voted and the unaffiliated who voted in the last general election, as well as those who have registered to vote since then. Obviously, in this situation you would disregard the Republicans because it is highly unlikely they would cross party lines and vote for you. That is, unless you feel there is a very compelling reason to spend money to try to get their vote.

Note: In larger elections, the above situations might be broken down into smaller units like wards or even precincts (election districts). After analysis, on a ward-by-ward or precinct-by-precinct basis, you will be able to further target the smaller areas in which you would want to spend the most time and money campaigning.

You would do well to go back and analyze the results of the past two elections for the position you are seeking, as well as all election results in the last two years or so in your area. Your time is better spent in areas that have historically voted for your party than in areas in which your party has gotten its laundry cleaned in election after election.

As you analyze, keep in mind that the area boundary of a precinct may have changed over the years, or some special situation may have occurred. Talk to local Republican and Democratic party officials, newspaper reporters and political junkies.

They often have insights that may not be evident from just looking at the hard numbers.

The Best Vote Getter?

The very best vote getter is the candidate himself or herself!

Register to Vote

In every community there are a large number of people who are not registered to vote. It is a personal opinion, but the time to conduct a voter registration drive is **not** in the midst of a campaign. I think it should be done during the off political season. It has been my experience that you will find some people in your travels who are interested in registering, but the number is minimal. Your time, once the campaign starts, is very valuable, and you have to be extremely careful how you spend it. You simply can't be everywhere doing everything. As a candidate, you need to be spending your time as productively as possible with people who have voted in the past and who probably will vote in your election.

You Need to Be Able to Count

About the first advice I ever received as a member of a City Council was that I need to be able to "count to five." We had eight members on the council, and to get something passed in most cases it took a majority of the members to agree and vote with you. In running for office, being able to count is also important. By analyzing past election results and the number of people registered, you will have a good idea of how many votes you will need to get elected. You have to do your homework and count.

The First Law

The best predictor of a voter's future behavior is his past behavior.

The Second Law

Older people are more motivated to vote than younger people.

One Vote

I'm sure you have all heard stories about an election being won by one vote. We had an election for a council seat that was won by two votes a couple of years ago, and another case of a person winning an election (or losing it, depending on which side you were on) by one vote just before that. As long as you are going to all the effort to win, it makes sense to give it all you've got.

Demographic and Attitude Research

In larger elections where there is much more money spent, it is common practice to do all kinds of very detailed research of the voter, his habits, his underlying feelings, etc. That is fine, and if you have the money, you will have the consultants knocking on your door to tell you all about how their services can win you the election. But this book is for the person who generally is not going to have the finances for that type of "big time" research.

Your Image in the Community IS Important

Many candidates are elected or defeated on the basis of a single piece of information. How often have you heard such comments as: "I like his style, I'm going to vote for him" or "She's been in office four years, and I haven't heard anything bad about her, so I think I will vote for her" or "That bad publicity has turned me off, I won't vote for him."

You Will *Not* Get Every Vote

It is not uncommon for a candidate who has died, or a candidate who has filed for a particular office, then never campaigned and moved out of state the next week to get as much as 20 to 25 percent of the vote in an election.

Voting Patterns

The candidates at the top of any ballot always receive the highest percentage of votes. If you go into a voting booth and you find a very long list of candidates for various offices, you can be sure that most voters will not have the patience to carefully go down the entire list. That is why you need to make your election important, regardless of where you are on the ballot. In some areas, I have seen campaigns whose main emphasis was something like, "Don't forget District 34 on the ballot." You need to be sure that your name and number are embedded in the voter's mind.

Voting Habits

Be aware of the social and economic precincts in every district. Different precincts have different concerns and voting habits.

What Is Important to Voters?

It's like the old story of the guy who says he makes all the **big** decisions in his household, and his wife makes all the small decisions. He decides whether he thinks the U.S.A. should be involved with NATO and whether he thinks we should cut back on spending for B-2 bombers. She decides where he should work, where the kids should go to school, what kind of car the family should own, etc.

The reason I point out this story is that regardless of the world situation, the things that most concern the average voter are the pocketbook and local issues. Never forget that.

Nonvoters

When a person is registered to vote and doesn't, you wonder why. Nobody has all the answers, but it is a fact that an exciting campaign that stimulates a lot of interest will bring more people to the polls.

Swing Districts

If in one election the voters in a particular district vote Republican and in the next election they vote Democrat or vice versa, you have a "swing" district. It would be worth the extra time and effort to keep this district for your party and your election.

Notary Public

In some states it is important that you be a notary public so you can register voters and notarize absentee ballots.

Women in Politics

The Republican National Committee and the Democratic National Committee both have extensive material that would be valuable for women (and men) who are seeking public office for the first time. Contact them in Washington. Check the bibliography in the back of this book for their address and phone number.

Nominating Petitions

You will need to gather a specific number of signatures from registered voters before your name will be put on the ballot. This requirement will vary from place to place. Check with your Secretary of State. You should always gather at least twice the number of signatures, even three times the needed amount for two reasons. First, many signatures are disallowed because the person signing is not registered (even though he thought he was), or the person signing lives out of the district, or a dead person came back to life and signed the petition. The second reason is that if a person signs your petition, you will hopefully have a supporter in the campaign. Stay in touch with petition signers, and to seal the deal, even consider sending them a thank you note.

Issue Research

Very simply, the reason you do issue research is to be sure you have your facts straight and you know what you are talking about. Done thoroughly, it establishes you as being competent and a serious candidate.

Never Forget Why You Are Running

The bottom line is: You want to have a say in the discussion and influence the decision-making on issues.

Significant Issues

In any campaign, the vast majority of voters are interested in only three or four issues. As a candidate, you must be up on those issues, know their background, possible solutions, know the pluses and the minuses of them, and have a strong stand (and your reasons why, with some specifics) on each of them, which you need to tell the voters over and over. After a voter has heard you, the ideal situation is for the voter to say to himself or herself, "Jimmy Jones has some good ideas that make sense."

Insignificant Issues

After the 1988 Bush vs. Dukakis campaign, someone made a comment that has stuck in my mind. It points out that what the people are thinking is important, not what *you* are thinking. The comment was, "Only people who have never shopped at K-Mart thought the Pledge of Allegiance and prison furloughs were insignificant issues." There is no such thing as 5.9 percent unemployed in this town. When you are unemployed, you're 100 percent unemployed.

One-issue Candidates

Whenever you hear someone talk about a one-issue candidate, most likely it is a person involved in the abortion issue, either pro-life or pro-choice. Some women are involved and care only about women's issues. There are candidates who are only concerned about environmental issues. These and many others are important to many individuals. But, to be elected by the voters to a position of authority, to be able to get elected and make a difference, you need to show that you are interested and competent in more than just one issue, because in this world there are many things that are important. And just because an issue is important to you doesn't mean your neighbors give a hoot about it. You need their vote, so you had better show interest in the issues that interest them.

Passion for Issues

Political gurus will tell you that when you move your position on an issue from being extreme to the middle, you lose passion for the issue.

The Media and the Issues

Like it or not, what the media focuses on is generally what they want people to have on their minds. Editorials influence what people think and are thinking. How—and if—protest meetings are reported will influence what people think. The media sets the agenda. What editors and news directors say is news is what you will read and hear about. And what you read about or hear about on the tube or radio may seem ridiculous, but it is still what is on people's minds and the subject of conversations because of the media coverage it has received. But how the issues are to be discussed and dealt with during a campaign is up to the candidate.

The media will talk an issue to death for a couple of weeks, then all of a sudden there is a new issue. And the cycle continues. Look back on the last year or so. How many major issues have the media been through? As you campaign, you will find that the pulse of the campaign will change accordingly. Be on the alert for how national issues will change the thinking of your voters on local issues.

Attending the Meetings

Before you get all excited about an issue, do more than read about it in the paper or hear about it on radio or TV. You need to do your homework, study the issue, talk to more than one knowledgeable person about the issue and, if it is a city issue, attend City Council meetings. If it is a county issue, attend meetings of the County Commission. If it is a school issue, attend school board meetings. Very often you will come away with a totally different perspective on it than what you read or heard. Some people get the idea they know it all after they read or hear a report on an issue. Maybe you know something about it, but every issue has at least two sides, and some issues have as many as 20 sides. As a candidate, don't go off half-cocked; make sure you know what you are talking about.

Hammer Away at *Your* Issue

Many politicians say the best advice they can give is to stay on the offensive, find a good issue, stick with it and hammer away at it over and over and over.

Don't Paint Yourself in a Corner

You will have people coming to you saying that if you support their position on an issue, you are sure to be elected. On the other hand, you will have people come to you who say that if you support a particular position, they will do everything in their power to get you defeated. You are not going to please everybody. You will **not** get everybody's vote. Choose your issues and stances carefully!

If you are approached about an issue, learn all you can about it, but **don't** make a commitment to support or oppose it. Some of the best advice I ever received was from Don Capper, an outstanding City Administrator, who told me when I was elected Mayor to not let myself get painted in a corner. He told me, "As sure as the sun comes up tomorrow, if you agree with one person or group on an issue, the opposing group with the opposing viewpoint will be in to see you and will have just as convincing arguments. They will want you to endorse their position, but you can't because you have painted yourself in a corner."

Some people just can't bring themselves around to the fact that there is always more than one side to an issue. Don't let anybody try to pressure you into taking a stand one way or the other until you know and have studied all the facts thoroughly and have looked at all sides of the issue. It is always best for you to say, "I need to study this issue, and I will before I take a stand on it."

Emotion and Issues

When you don't have real important issues in an election or strong personalities, most often symbols work better than substance in gaining voter support. In other words, emotions can often work better in campaigns than issues.

The Main Issue, the Only Issue

The only real issue in any race is which candidate can do the best job if elected.

The voter decides who can do the best job by considering what we call issues. I think most voters say to themselves, "Which candidate will feel more like I do in relation to an issue?" And if a voter agrees with you on most issues, he or she probably believes you are the person who can do the best job. Sometimes what you specifically propose to do about a problem is not as important to many people as the fact that you are concerned and care about it.

Issue Research

You need to know the issues backward and forward, all the ins and outs, and all the possible solutions. You need to be ready with accurate and informed answers from your research.

Position Papers (White Papers)

From research on the issues, some candidates issue position papers (sometimes referred to as "white papers") which, as the name implies, state your position on a particular issue. The size of your campaign will determine how much research you will do and if you need to issue such a paper. In some campaigns I have seen them issued only on specific issues, and only after an attack by the opponent.

I think you would do well to write a paper every two weeks or so on a different issue. It will get you press, and it will keep interest in the campaign, especially if you can come up with creative solutions to problems that catch the eye and ear of the media.

Position papers are generally only given to the media, or to some especially interested citizens. Make them short—a single page is ideal—and to the point. Don't get too windy! And it is not necessary to cover every single detail.

Opposition Research

How vulnerable is your opponent? Every candidate has strengths as well as weaknesses. You had better find out what they are with your opponent because I'm telling you that he or she is researching to find out what *your* strengths and weaknesses are.

When you research your opponent, it isn't that you are only interested in digging up dirt. You are interested in the differences that exist between you and your opponent as far as issues are concerned, backgrounds, activism, philosophy, education, work record, community involvement, political involvement, past votes on issues, past achievements and awards, leadership positions, character, etc.

The idea is to use the information you have gathered to keep your opponent on the defensive. If you have areas where you are strong and he or she is weak, mention them at every opportunity. It is advisable to keep a file on each and every item, clipping, rumor, hearsay, etc., about your opponent in the campaign manager's office for ready reference at a moment's notice. Larger campaigns will hire a clipping service to clip all articles from the papers regarding your opponent for a fee. There are also audio and video clipping services that will send you tapes of stories about you and your opponent for a fee. Most people these days have a VCR. Have one of your volunteers tape newscasts with stories about the campaign for the file.

Chapter 12

Issues

▼

The Best Advice from
U.S. Senator Frank H. Murkowski of Alaska

"My advice is simply to work like heck during election years. Not to forget that a voter's opinion of you is formed in each individual town in your state. I am a firm believer in doing all the television and radio that you can afford, but also in putting up more yard signs than your opponent and in visiting as many of your likely voter strongholds as possible, meeting people and listening to their views—listening being more important than talking most of the time.

Another piece of advice is that once you get elected, always answer your mail, and really push your staff to do a great job of helping constituents with their problems. Handling the federal or state or local bureaucracy is no easy task. I still find I get as much satisfaction out of pushing the bureaucracy to do something for an individual constituent, as I do from passing major legislation in the Senate. When I stop feeling that way, I know it will be time for me to do something else."

▲ ▲

The person in charge of issues will research and help the candidate develop the issues to his or her advantage.

Just What Are the Issues?

You can commission an expensive survey of the voters in your area, you can discuss the matter with your steering committee members, or you can just be alert and keep your ear to the ground and look for things that are bugging people. Your volunteers canvassing door to door and over the phone, gathering signatures for a filing petition, etc., will pick up many tidbits of information about the voters' thoughts on issues. That is informal research, but generally it is good street-smart research. As you, the candidate, go door to door, it won't take long to find out what the *true* issues are in the campaign. Whatever they are, you need to know the issues that are important to the voters. Sure, there will be some very specific issues in some specific areas or neighborhoods, but I'm talking about general issues that most of the voters (if they are concerned at all) are interested in.

The size of your campaign will determine what route you take.

Obviously, if you can afford good professional research, do it. If you can't, even a survey done anonymously by your volunteers of more than 300 or so randomly selected voters in your area would be very worthwhile. Questions could be asked regarding your name recognition vs. your opponent and other local officials, as well as a question about the voter's concerns. The obvious reason to do this survey anonymously is that if they know they are being asked the question by a member of your campaign, they will be sure to tell the interviewer that you are a wonderful human being. If they don't know who is calling, they might be honest and give a different sort of opinion, and you might learn something. And that is what you want.

I've done this, and it is extremely enlightening, especially if people on your steering committee or even you think everybody knows and loves you.

You might contact the Political Science Department at a local college. Maybe they would conduct a survey as a class project, and you could throw a pizza party for them to say thanks.

How to Find Out

Don't just take the advice of your cronies who hang around campaign headquarters, or your opinionated brother-in-law.

You need to get out amongst the folks and find out what they think and are concerned about.

Get Elected, Make a Difference!

Voter talking to Rich on campaign trail.

Chapter 13

Grass-roots Campaigning

▼

***The Best Advice from
Congressman Ray LaHood of Illinois***

"There are two pieces of advice that I would give to anyone running for public office. First, know what your most strongly held beliefs are, in order to be able to articulate them, and do not be dissuaded by your critics or the media. Secondly, if you listen 90 percent of the time, you can learn a great deal more about how to solve problems."

Believe me, I know a few things about grass-roots campaigning. As a candidate for Mayor, I personally knocked on the door of every registered voter in our town asking for support. And recently when I ran as an extreme underdog candidate for Governor of Kansas, I conducted the most extensive grass-roots campaign in the history of the state.

If you have a lot of volunteers, they can assist you in your door-to-door effort. They can also pass out your literature, send notes to people, make phone calls, put up yard signs, etc. Nothing beats repeated contact with targeted voters by you and your volunteers. These are the undecided voters whom you need to nudge into voting for you.

Canvasser

Canvassing is the process of either going door to door or doing a phone survey, either by the candidate or volunteers, to the homes of all registered voters in the district, division or block, whatever it is known by in your area. You want to find out who is likely to vote for the candidate. Each voter in each home is given a rating:

- 1 if a supporter
- 2 if leaning toward candidate
- 3 if undecided
- 4 if leaning against candidate
- 5 if supporting someone else

Smile, give a pleasant greeting, make the call brief, and leave campaign literature. Usually the best time to make calls is from 7 to 9 p.m. during the week, and on Saturday and Sunday afternoons from 1 until 5 p.m.

Since most people will tell you what they think you want to hear, this is not an exact science. If a person knows that you are a representative of Candidate "A," he or she will probably tell you that they support Candidate "A." That is why most phone surveyors do not identify the candidate they are phoning for. You could be seriously fooling yourself unless you get honest opinions.

In a primary election, you would only canvass those registered voters who are eligible to vote in *that* election.

In a general election, you canvass all registered voters. Many people do not vote strictly party line; they vote "for the person." So in a partisan general election, while most Republicans would vote for a Republican candidate and vice versa, there are always those who cross party lines for whatever reason and vote for the candidate of the other party. Still, your best bet is to concentrate on the people in your party and the independent voters who are leaning toward you.

When canvassing, the question is generally phrased this way: "Irv Hoffman and Betty Doe are running for Mayor of Smithville this year. Which candidate will you probably vote for?" From their responses, you will be able to give them a 1, 2, 3, 4 or 5 rating. This rating is noted on a 3" x 5" card for each voter, or on a computer data base. If the person you are talking with seems receptive at all, it is wise to also ask, "What are the issues you are most concerned about?" Their answer should be noted on the card or in the data file in the computer.

You should basically concentrate on the 1, 2 and 3's. Don't waste your time or mailings on the 4 or 5's; they are the least likely to be persuaded to vote for you. The prime object is to turn the 2's and 3's into 1's and get them to the polls on election day. It's that simple and that complicated.

Canvassing is usually started about six weeks before the election, depending on the size of the district and the number of volunteers available to help canvass. It is then continued up until election day. As a person's rating changes, it should be changed on their card or computer data file.

Everyone who is doing the canvassing should agree on how the rating system works if you are to have a true indication of how people feel about your candidacy.

Note: These calls to find a person's opinions must be made anonymously. It is not the intention to have the canvassers identify themselves as working for your campaign and answer campaign questions about the candidate's stand on issues.

If you knock on someone's door or call when they are in the middle of a meal, smile, beg off, excuse yourself and tell them you will contact them later. You don't want to annoy anyone. That is good ol' common courtesy. Good common sense should always prevail.

Don't make notes in the presence of the person you are talking with. Get out your pen after they shut the door and you have walked away from the house.

You don't have to rush your conversation, but do make it brief, smile, say thank you, turn around and leave. Don't linger! (Have you ever noticed how some people just can't find the way to say good-bye and leave?) Whether you are the candidate or a volunteer, you need to move on. You have more people to see and talk with. Some conversations last 20 seconds, some may last 10 minutes. That is long enough.

On many occasions you will be invited to come in and have a cup of coffee, a drink or a soda. It is best to pass and gracefully ask for a raincheck. You have a lot of ground to cover.

Volunteers working in pairs, a man and a woman, seem to work best for volunteers going door to door. Volunteers who are not related work better than married couples.

Selling Yourself

Everybody has different ideas of how to run for office. They may not want to run themselves, but they offer an abundant supply of free advice. Regardless, it all boils down to the fact that to be elected, you have to sell yourself and your ideas to the electorate, and they have to buy them. Being an old peddler myself, I can tell you that you don't sell everybody, and you had better be mentally ready to hear people say such things as, "That is the dumbest idea I have ever heard," or, "You wanting to represent me, you've got to be kidding!" or "There is no way on this earth that I would support you," or "Not only am I not going to support you, I'm going to do all in my power to make sure that you are not elected," etc. I realize that to hear people say things like that doesn't give you a very good feeling, but you had best just grin and bear it. You will survive and, in the end, you will hopefully find that you have more supporters than detractors, and if you can find one more vote than your opponent, you win.

If you have been around for a while and have had considerable dealings with people, you know that not everybody loves you, and the old statement is true, "Friends come and go, but enemies hang around forever."

You're running for office because you have had the guts to speak out on public issues, you are somewhat knowledgeable about the issues, and you have made some friends who agree with you and encourage you to seek public office.

Are you—and what you stand for and offer—what the voters are looking for?

What Is the #1 Determining Factor on Why People Vote the Way They Do?

After all is said and done, everybody is concerned about themselves first. How will your election personally benefit them. Period.

Mentally Rehearsing (Visualization)

Exceptional athletes, exceptional speakers and exceptional politicians mentally rehearse their actions in advance. As a candidate, it is important for you to go over in your mind what you want to say and do and accomplish *before* an event. Maybe it is what point you want to emphasize at the afternoon coffee, or the new proposal you have that you want to get across in an interview with the reporter. Rehearse what questions might be asked, or as you go door to door, what point you want to get across to this particular voter, etc. It is nothing more than smart planning that will pay huge dividends.

Speaking Before Groups

I know it is tough, but you absolutely must keep yourself from getting too windy. Audiences appreciate it if you talk for less time than they thought you would or should, and many a candidate has lost voters by going on and on and on. Make a point, then sit down.

And be careful about "winging" answers. It can get you in big trouble. If you are asked a question you are not prepared to intelligently answer, say so. "I don't have an answer for that right now. I'm working on it (and, in fact, you are, effective immediately) and will have something to say about it soon."

Remembering Names and Faces

It's tough, but you have to make a conscious, serious effort. Most people realize that as you campaign you will meet many people, and it is impossible to remember all their names. But you have to try. A trick, if there is a trick that works to help remember people's names, is to engage them in some kind of conversation and find out something about them or their business that is unique. Oftentimes I have found that will help me remember them, and occasionally I can pull up a correct name. At least I try.

Introductions

When you meet someone, stick out your hand and say, "Hi, I'm Dave Stephens" or "I'm Irv Hoffman." Most people will respond by saying something like, "I'm Lou Serrone," or "I'm Jane Klein." Then you say something like, "Jane (it is important to repeat their name so it sticks in your mind), it's great to meet you. What the heck are you doing in a place like this?" or, "I understand that this organization would never have gotten off the ground without all your hard work." That will get the conversation going. Don't just say "Hello" and stand there. Find out that person's name and repeat it and be friendly and human. You may have just met and gotten to know a person who may become a great friend.

Some Basic Thoughts About Grass-roots Campaigning

Know your area or district in detail. Get to know the people, their problems and concerns.

This is a people business. People dealing with people. Don't come across with a "know-it-all" attitude.

Very few people get up in the morning and say, "I just can't wait for the next political campaign to start." Frankly, elections aren't very important to most people. That is why you have to repeat your message over and over and over to get them to do what you want—vote for you.

Be sincere when talking to the voters.

Each day is a learning experience. Anticipate questions that you may be asked, and be prepared to give people *short* answers.

No candidate ever lost an election because he or she started too early.

Be prepared to counter any attack from your opponent. Let good old common sense prevail. You should have a good idea of what your opponent is going to attack you with. Nobody's perfect, so simply accept your liabilities and accentuate your assets. Have your plan of action ready, or maybe even be proactive, talk about it yourself and preempt and take the steam out of the attack.

People want personal attention. Say thank you, thank you, thank you, and I care, I care, I care. And mean it!

First impressions count!

Always consider before you commit. You need to keep in mind the question, "Will this help me get more votes?" "Is this the most efficient use of my time, energy and resources?"

Your time is precious. You need your best efforts to get elected; don't spend time on anything unless it means votes.

Act like a candidate. You need to walk and talk and act and stand tall and be enthusiastic and interested like a candidate should be. Always take a genuine interest in others and really care about their feelings whether you are in a political race or not.

The voters want to personally meet and look the candidate in the eye. That can be done only by you. Personal contact is especially important and expected in most local races. Don't be fooled into thinking that your stories in the paper or your mailings or the short blurb on TV is just as good. These things aren't. Nothing beats personal contact.

Campaigns are more often lost than won. Errors made by one camp and taken advantage of by the opposition can turn certain victory into defeat and vice versa. In any campaign, you need to think before you act.

Voters have short attention spans. They don't follow government and politics the way you do, and they don't want to. You're dreaming if you think the average family is going to sit around the dinner table and have a serious discussion of your "five-point plan." If you are going to talk to them about the election, you had better make it short and sweet.

Don't overtalk! In your literature, in interviews going door to door, don't get too windy. As the old saying goes, when they ask you what time it is, tell them what time it is, not how to make a watch.

Smile! It works wonders.

In every campaign, on any issue, let good old common horse sense prevail.

The media is **not** your enemy. By communicating with the members of the media, you will most generally find they may be opinionated (and so are you), but fair.

Be prepared for the "eleventh-hour sneak attack," or what we call in my home town, the "green light special," the day before the election. Have a plan ready to immediately counter such an attack.

Timing is important. Plan for your campaign to peak on election day. That is easier to talk about than to do, but it should be a goal to work toward.

Get-out-the-vote efforts are so very important. For most people, your election, the fact that there is an election, is **not** the most important thing in their lives. You need to impose on people for a few minutes to vote.

Keep in mind that many voters don't decide who to vote for until they walk into the voting booth. Your last-minute, election-day efforts can pay dividends. The last-minute phone calls, the yard signs, the ads, etc. This is when those things pay off. Now that you have the ball on the five-yard line, don't fumble it; take it across the goal line. Don't think you have the election in the bag. I personally have seen friends lose by just a few votes. Make the extra effort! You'll be glad you did.

Most people vote for people, not necessarily for the political party to which they belong.

A political election is a one-day sale that had better be successful.

In your campaign, accentuate the positive.

Talk the language of the person you are talking with. The conversation will be necessarily different when talking to an

Grass-roots Campaigning

inner city voter than to a farmer. You need to talk in terms of the other person's interests, and be careful what you say. I'm reminded of the story of the Presidential candidate who asked the Iowa farmer: "How much wool are you planting this year?"

Try to avoid talking excessively about yourself and what you want or what you have done. The word "you" is more important than "I." (I have a friend who says, "Don't talk about yourself because we will talk about you when you are gone.")

Always observe the Golden Rule: "Do unto others as you would have them do unto you."

As I heard a basketball coach say on TV one time, there is a big difference between showing up to play, and showing up to **win!** The difference is attitude.

Don't ever let it be said by anybody that you didn't ask for their vote.

Most voters have never been personally contacted by a candidate. It can be very beneficial to get together with a number of volunteers and organize or take part in some community project. I have seen this work especially well in creating good will and name ID when the volunteers are wearing T-shirts with the candidate's name on them. Remember, you want to do these things because they are the right thing to do, and not just because you are involved in a political campaign. If you have a history of involvement, you are way ahead of the game. As the saying goes, the best indicator of your future performance is your past performance.

As you go door to door, make sure you carry literature to hand to the resident. If the voter is not home, be sure to leave a piece of literature on the door on which you have written something like: "Sorry I missed you when I stopped by today. I would appreciate your vote for Sheriff on May 22nd. Sincerely, Larry McAulay."

In a conversation with a voter, talk about what the voter wants to talk about, **not** what you want to talk about.

Don't tell ethnic jokes to anybody, and don't bad-mouth your town or area. Regardless of how bad you might think it is, it is the source of pride to many people. Talk optimistically about how the area can be even better.

Send a thank you note to everybody who signed your nominating petition.

You as the candidate set the tone for the election.

Contact undecided voters more than one time, in person, via the phone and mailings spaced over a period of time. Keep selling.

Don't react too quickly to criticism.

In grass-roots campaigning, remember, as the commercial says, you can phone it there, you can fax it there, you can mail it there, but nothing beats your being there.

Do newsworthy things.

As you go door to door or canvass over the phone, find out if anybody needs an absentee ballot. If they do, make the necessary arrangements for them.

If you go door to door, you have to do it with brute force. It is not something that most people feel comfortable about doing. My first selling job years ago was selling subscriptions to the *Wall Street Journal* door to door in office buildings in downtown St. Louis. Each morning I would go downtown, pick up that morning's paper, and before I had the nerve to walk into the first office, I would walk around the block the building was on four or five times to get up the nerve to go into the first office. Once I did, I was rolling, and it became easier with each passing day.

It is a little like public speaking. It will scare the devil out of you initially, but the more you do it, the more comfortable you feel.

Never give a person an answer to a question or problem unless you have a prepared answer. Don't just blurt out something off the top of your head.

As you go door to door, you will be amazed to find that almost every house has a pet. And the first time you ring a bell and a giant Great Dane comes flying up to the door and looks at you through the glass, it will be a thrill you will never forget.

If you just can't bring yourself to go door to door by yourself, take a friend with you. (Don't take young kids with you.)

Only go door to door of voters *who are registered to vote.* I repeat, only go door to door of the voters who are registered to vote in the upcoming election. Your local election office can supply you with an up-to-date list of the registered voters in your area. I've done some personal research of my experiences, and I have found that almost every time the person who has the most to say, the person who is the most negative about everything, is usually not even registered to vote. Don't waste your time with them. And remember, you are not putting on a voter registration drive. You need to go where the registered voters are and convince them to vote for you. This is how you need to spend your time.

As you go door to door, you are going to meet some of the nicest human beings on earth, and you will make new friends. But you need to be careful that you don't keep the conversations going too long at the moment, because you have places to go and people to see.

As you make the rounds, you will make note of individuals whom you will want to eliminate from your mailing list.

Be sure you know the address of the polling place of each home you visit and tell them.

"The bee that gets the honey doesn't hang around the hive." Get out of your campaign headquarters and see the people. Let somebody else stuff envelopes and do mailings. Your job is to have direct contact with as many voters as possible. If you don't have better things to do than to stuff envelopes, then you are a lousy candidate.

Great Advice

When people ask a candidate a question, they don't want to know what you *think,* they want to know what you're *like.*

Literature Drops

Carefully control who distributes your door-to-door literature and how it is distributed. If you don't, you'll hear from people upset about your campaign literature littering the neighborhood or the fact that the person delivering the literature walked on their lawn or flower bed.

High School/College Credit

Some teachers/professors give students extra credit if they participate in a campaign. You might find some excellent volunteer help in this manner.

Negative Campaigning

One fundamental fact of psychology is that negative information is more deeply imbedded in the mind than positive information. Sure, most people have a great dislike for the stuff, but the real point is that people do absorb it like a sponge.

A Positive Campaign

It has always been my policy in campaigns to say to my opponent at the start, "I'm going to run a positive campaign, and I hope you choose to do the same. But please be forewarned, if somebody starts a negative campaign against me, the war is on." (Remember, comparing your record with your opponent's record is **not** negative campaigning.)

Campaign Workers

There are a surprising number of people out there—seniors, youth, homemakers, businessmen and women, students—whom you can recruit to work on your campaign. But you have to **ask** them.

Campaign Rally

Hold it the day or so before the election. Invite the media and the world. Have it in a place that is way too small. You want people fighting to get in and people standing in the halls. You want the parking lot jammed to capacity. You want this to be the big event, the place to be. You need a band, banners, signs (printed and homemade), and one or two fired-up speakers preceding the candidate. Remember, the candidate is the show. Don't have some famous band there and find out that the people have come to hear the band, and not the candidate.

Parades

If you are going to have a parade, make sure you have a parade permit. If you are going to ride in more than one parade in separate communities on, say, the 4th of July, see if you can arrange to be in the early stages of the first parade and the later stages of the second parade. That way, some candidates are in more than one parade on the same morning if the communities are not too far apart.

Being on Time

There is nothing more frustrating to people who plan events than to have you arrive late. You will make great friends by making sure you can adhere to a tight schedule.

Street Rallies

In some areas, the candidate and supporters will gather at a street corner with signs and banners and pennants and flags and wave and hand out literature to passing motorists and pedestrians. Then the candidate will give a short, fast, punchy, pump-'em-up talk to keep the enthusiasm going. In the week preceding the rally, flyers announcing the event are distributed and stapled on boards all over the neighborhood. Sometimes a candidate will hire a sound truck to go around the neighborhood announcing the event.

Video Parties

In recent years, some candidates have produced a short video, had hundreds of copies made, and distributed them to volunteers with the idea that they would invite some of their friends over for coffee or drinks and show them the video about you and your campaign.

Coffees

I'm not a big fan of "coffees." They sound good, but it has been my experience that the people who can be convinced to come to them are your friends and supporters already.

Receptions

Now I do like receptions. Hold it like from 5 to 7 in the evening during the week. Have some drinks, some food. Charge to get in. Talk a little politics early. Then later in the evening pitch for more money. Have a good friend, a strong member of your steering committee, arrange one at a nice place. I'm not talking about an expensive place; I'm talking about a nice place. In our area, a local beer distributor has a meeting room that they allow groups to use. It's just big enough. The idea is always to have an event in a room that is too small for the anticipated crowd. You always want the room or hall or auditorium overflowing. There is nothing worse than to have a crowd of 50 people in a room that will hold 500 people. It looks like your event is a failure. What you want is people who can't get in and you have to pipe the talk outside, or put chairs in the hallway so the fire marshal will come in and tell you that you have to clear the hallways. It is great for publicity for the candidate. It is human nature that people always want to go to places that are sold out and you have to stand in line and wait to get in like some baseball, basketball, football games, restaurants and movies. Events that are standing room only are great for a campaign.

You want the place packed like sardines. Then you have one of the elements of a successful event. It will be impressive and maddening to your supporters, and they will raise hell with you about it after it is over, but they will love it and talk about it for a long time. They will tell everybody in sight that your reception was packed to the gills. And there were so many people you could hardly get in the door. That's great publicity. It is great to be involved with a winner. It's like Yogi used to say, "It's so crowded nobody ever goes there."

Send invitations to supporters and undecideds and make phone calls. Don't bet on R.S.V.P.'s, because most people ignore them these days. How many people will show up will depend on the list of people you invite, but you hope that 10 percent of those invited walk through the door.

Be sure that you have "stuff" for the attendees like buttons, peel-off stickers, name tags (don't forget name tags, because you want to be sure that all your friends and supporters know all the other friends and supporters).

Other events—to name just a few that are used to get your supporters together—are barbecues, watermelon feeds, picnics, backyard parties, lunches and dinners of all sorts.

Churches

It helps to have good contact with ministers, priests and rabbis in the community. Don't expect them to get up on the pulpit and endorse your candidacy, but they do have contact with and influence many people in the community. If they agree with your message and your stands, they can do you a lot of good.

Civic Clubs, Etc.

Arrange to speak to all your civic clubs, breakfast clubs, etc. These are the leaders in the community, the movers and shakers, and they need to hear from you.

Questions and My Answers About Ethics

In a party system dominated by special interests, how does the elected official maintain integrity?

Name me one group that *isn't* special interest. Everybody promotes their own program. Who is to determine what is best? Who is to say if it is better to paint the wall blue or to paint it beige?

How do special interest groups affect you?

You have to listen to everybody and put everything in its proper perspective.

How does an elected official maintain integrity, yet remain answerable to constituents?

I'm open to everybody. I talk to everybody. I gather all the facts, and I make a decision.

How does a politician who raises money from the public and special interest groups vote when the vote affects the group who has given the dollars?

On the merits of the issue.

How does the need to raise money affect your decisions?

Without money you have nothing. You cannot be involved unless, of course, you are willing to spend your own money. People who believe you are fair and balanced will give you money for your campaign. They agree philosophically with what you are trying to accomplish. That's the system. You live with it. It doesn't affect decisions, but it is necessary.

What is the balance of personal ego with the political process and getting things done for your constituency?

My heart is in the right place. You have to be willing to put your heart and soul into the decisions you make. You try to do good, and you try to get some things done. I do what I feel is right and fair, and I sleep like a baby at night.

All these questions were asked at a political training session for Chamber of Commerce members. All the questions seem to give the impression that getting dollars to conduct campaigns corrupts elected officials.

I have a real problem with that. It helps perpetuate the impression that all elected officials are dishonest, and I resent that very much. People are basically honest; it is just that some feel that if a politician doesn't agree with you on a matter, that he or she is crooked and dishonest.

The Customer (the Voter) Is Always Right

That might be the policy at the grocery store, but in politics, quite often the voter isn't even close to having the facts straight on so many matters. Unfortunately, too many voters form their opinions after hearing a one-liner on radio or TV or reading a headline in the paper.

Phone Bank

Phone lines need to be ordered, and generally phoning is done from a quiet area of headquarters. Phone bank volunteers generally work from a prepared script to ascertain from voters their feeling toward the candidate. The job of the phone solicitor is not to sell the candidate or to argue with the person they are calling. It is to give out information and to collect information.

Advance Men and Women

Their job is to make sure all events and appearances run as smoothly as possible. These people are needed only in larger campaigns. In those campaigns, it is a job for an experienced person, not a novice.

You have to exercise some political smarts to make sure the candidate's appearance is maximized and is pulled off without a hitch.

There are horror stories of microphones not working, events being scheduled at a time in conflict with another big event, appearances being scheduled outdoors with no contingency plan in case of bad weather, etc. Make sure these things don't happen to you.

Field Supervisor

This person oversees everything going on outside campaign headquarters. He or she makes sure everything is covered and running smoothly and all the details are being taken care of by those assigned to do them.

Voter Registration of New Residents

As you come across new residents of your area in your travels and involvement in the community, make sure to get them registered to vote. It might do you well to have a flyer typed up and copied that would list all the particulars on getting registered. New people do move in and out of communities all the time. In a conversation with them, you will find out real fast if they have any interest. And while you are at it, without being too boastful, tell them about how good a job you have done in the past in the community and will do in the future if elected.

Scheduler

This person and this person only, *let me repeat,* this person and this person only, and only after consultation with the candidate, is to make commitments regarding the candidate. This person, and this person only, is in charge of the master calendar of events and appearances of the candidate. The scheduler arranges and then confirms the candidate's appearances. Not even the candidate should make commitments without consulting the scheduler.

You will find that as soon as you become a candidate, you will begin to receive invitations to an unbelievable number of events. At these events you may have the opportunity to meet the folks, or you may be invited to speak. These appearances will range from a coffee at someone's home to a debate or forum. The scheduler needs to be a person with a political sense who is not too quick to accept. Many a candidate has been bad-mouthed because the scheduler said the candidate would attend, only to find out later that the candidate canceled so he or she could attend a "bigger" deal. Make sure that everybody understands that if you make a commitment, you will make it in writing.

Don't make commitments too far in advance, and be very careful about commitments to debates and forums. The scheduler needs to work very, very closely with the campaign manager to make sure that the overall campaign plan and strategy is being followed for maximum positive exposure for the candidate.

The scheduler must at all times remember that the candidate must maximize his or her time. You can't spend two hours at a coffee with six people when you could be talking to a homeowners' association with 250 people in attendance. You have to go where the votes are.

Speakers Bureau

In candidate elections, the speaker most people want to hear is the candidate. In issue elections, a speakers bureau is very effective, where you would line up knowledgeable speakers on the subject to speak before all kinds of clubs and organizations whose members would be voting on the issue.

In our county we recently had an issue election. One member of the steering committee was in charge of lining up clubs and organizations where our speakers could talk about the issue. It worked beautifully, and the issue passed.

Special Projects

In every campaign, there are special projects that show up and need to be taken care of. A picnic, a rally, a special dinner, etc. You need an all-around person to handle these as they come up.

Motivators

Voting is emotional. The leading favorite motivators are Fear, Hope, Hate or Love.

Voters Are Motivated by Three Basic Concerns

1. His or her pocketbook
2. His or her family
3. How he or she spends their leisure time

An issue like "fear of crime" impacts all three of these basic concerns.

Who votes for whom is not an exact science, but it is generally agreed that people vote for candidates who make them feel good, and people vote for the candidate they think can do the best job.

How they vote is an emotional decision. That is why you have all the appeals to our patriotism and our fear of crime in every election.

Rich and Nancy Becker (in van) campaigning in Kansas.

Chapter 14

Get Exposure/Advertising/Publicity

▼

The Best Advice from
U.S. Senator Paul David Wellstone of Minnesota

"1. Capture the imagination of people.

2. Do not come across as a 'hack attack' politician.

3. Be honest.

4. Focus on economic justice issues."

Press Secretary

This is the person who handles communication with the media. He or she can speak for the candidate and the campaign. Often, in smaller campaigns, the candidate acts as his or her own press secretary. Don't try to outguess what the press will be interested in. Over and over in my years as an elected official and as a candidate, I have been called by friends in the media about things out of the blue. You will find that what a reporter or an editor feels is important is often much different than what you feel is important or relevant to the campaign.

This person should be familiar with the media and work with them to be sure the candidate's message is delivered in its best light. In the absence of the candidate, many campaign questions can be answered by the press secretary, using his or her good judgment.

You need to press on and try to present the candidate's perspective on the issues. Make sure the information is accurate, and be sure your press secretary can be considered a good reliable source of information for the media.

Communications

The field of communications covers a wide area. Its covers media advertising, news releases, dealing with reporters, yard signs, etc. It deals with all the things necessary for you to get exposure, to get name recognition, to get elected.

Approximately 60 to 80 percent of your budget should be spent in this area. A number of your steering committee members will be specifically involved in the communications aspect of your campaign. It is critical that all these members work together in harmony to get the job done. The very last place you need confusion is in communicating your message.

Everything you do with respect to communications is directed toward getting your message, *the same basic message,* repeated over and over to the media and the public. It is important that you come across as "down-home," direct, candid and unrehearsed. That is another way of saying that you don't want to be, or to appear, phony.

Basic Rule of Communication

Experts say that in face-to-face meetings, only 7 percent of an audience's interpretation of our message comes from our words, 38 percent from what we hear in tone of voice and voice inflections, but 55 percent from what we see. In total, 93 percent of what we communicate in person comes from the nonverbal portion of our message.

Coordination of Material and Message

What voters hear about you is what they tend to remember first. And each time your message is repeated (and you can repeat your simple basic message a hundred different ways), it should be mutually reinforcing all the good things that the voters are saying about you.

Writing Memos

When you write memos to your people, be sure they are:

1. Complete
2. Concise
3. Clear

The memos should always say "Thank You" in advance of any action that you request.

Some Rules and Tips About Communications

Communicate with energy and enthusiasm.

Be an interesting individual. It comes across that you have a broad range of interests.

Be committed to your cause.

Have a willingness to take clear stands on issues not always popular with the audience.

People follow people they consider to be leaders.

Your message must be completed quickly because people have short attention spans.

People use generalities and jump to conclusions.

People resist changes, so avoid the word "change," and call it something else, but still change it.

Be comfortable, make others comfortable. Lighten up. Take your candidacy seriously, but don't take yourself so seriously.

Try to be a "nice person." If you are liked, people will forgive your faults.

When you talk to people, try to paint word pictures instead of just saying words.

Know what you are talking about. You don't have to be an expert on everything, but people want to feel that you know more about the subject than they do.

Create a sense of urgency in your communications since people react best under pressure.

People hide uncomplimentary attitudes, so don't take everybody's opinions too seriously.

People don't want to know every little detail about you. There is nothing wrong with a little mystery. People are suspicious of those who think they are perfect.

Get Exposure/Advertising/Publicity

To lead, you have to communicate. I heard a baseball manager say one time that he had no intention of managing anyone. He said he intended to communicate with everyone.

People glance instead of read. That is one reason that I like to put my name in big bold letters on each side of a flyer that I hand out or mail. Even if a person glances at it and promptly throws it in the trash, that person has seen your name and hopefully it will stick in their subconscious.

You will always have new people to contact and talk to since many people change residences each year. Check lists that you buy, rent, borrow or whatever to communicate with potential voters. Some are 90 percent up to date, some are 30 percent accurate.

In communications, in person and by mail, people respond to emotional appeals, the warmth of good sentiment.

People want to be sought after and talked to. As Mayor, I was available to talk to people all the time, but I had one special day each year when I personally invited all the citizens to City Hall to sit across the table from me and personally tell me their thoughts, feelings and concerns about the city.

People like to see their names and their pictures in the paper, on TV and mentioned on the radio. And people love to have their picture taken. For years I have taken my camera to every city event and have taken thousands of photos which, in turn, I have given to those whom I could identify. It is a great "shtick."

Incumbents

We have all heard the tales over and over about how difficult it is to beat an incumbent. It is true that the incumbent has a leg up on everybody else. But, take heart, incumbents are being beaten every day by candidates who are closer to the people, who are using creative communications and modern technology to maximize their time and the impact of their message.

Name Recognition (Name ID)

Voters need to know your name, even if they have never personally met you. They must recognize you name, and they must hear and see your name over and over in a campaign in a good positive light. That is an absolute must if you are to be elected. So you need to pull out all the stops in this regard.

It has been reported that a challenger who won, among other things, produced a radio and TV spot that had his name mentioned nine times in 30 seconds.

There is no guarantee that once a person knows who you are that they are going to like you or vote for you. But you have to have the confidence that they will.

Appearing at Functions

As a candidate, you will be asked to appear at all kinds of functions, at all hours, for all kinds of reasons. Often they have no relation to the campaign in any way, shape or form. As a candidate, I have been to functions that had more candidates in attendance than voters. Every appearance, any action you take has to be done with the idea of maximizing the number of potential votes in relation to the time and energy you devote to it.

You'll have to analyze the situation, but most times it is important to limit your appearance to making a very short talk, shaking plenty of hands, and then leave. If you spend a lot of time standing around with your hands in your pockets, you're making a big mistake. You need to send the message that you have places to go and people to see. You need, in fact, to get out and keep moving and keep meeting people. It is very important to be visible, but it is also important to keep moving.

Publicity

Publicity is advertising that you don't have to pay for. A positive story about you in the paper is better and more believable than any ad you could buy.

Without question, good publicity is the most effective way to establish identity, tell your story and motivate the voter to vote for you.

The News Release/The Press Release/The Publicity Release

Whatever you call it, it serves the same function. The classic definition of a press release is a message to the newspapers. While many people still call them press releases, I believe the more accepted term these days, to cover all media, is to call it a news release. Many members of the electronic media (radio, TV, cable) couldn't care less about receiving press releases. In this book I'll call them news releases.

Tips on Writing, Preparing, Sending, Using, Getting the Most Impact from Your News Releases

- *Double-space* your typed (never handwritten) release.
- Use 8-1/2" x 11" paper and only on *one* side.
- At the top, put in capital letters, **"For Immediate Release"** (unless there is a very compelling reason to put a specific date and time for release of the information).
- At the top you should prominently have your committee name, address, city, state, zip, phone number and fax number.
- Before you get into the body of the copy, write a short headline at the top that gives the reader an idea of what the release is about. Such as "Linver visits nursing home to talk about health care."
- Newspapers love names. The more names you have in your news release, the better chance it has of being used. So don't be shy about using the names of the prominent individuals on your steering committee.
- Have wide margins on each side.
- Don't staple the pages together, use a paper clip.
- Keep the paragraphs short.
- The first paragraph, the lead paragraph, is so very important. It should contain the answers to the question: Who? What? Where? When? Why? and possibly How? It should have all the basic information and be

a synopsis of the whole release. The rest of the paragraphs should deal with the details that are also important in descending order.

- Get to the point. Don't get too windy!
- Use simple language and short sentences.
- Never forget that the media are always looking for story suggestions.
- Don't try to cover more than one issue in a release. Save your stand on the other issues and send them out separately about a week or so apart.
- If you have a chance to include the name of a prominent individual in the community in your release, do it.
- In each and every news release, emphasize your theme. Remember there are hundreds of ways to say the same thing over and over.
- If possible, keep your release to one sheet. If more than one page, put "...more..." at bottom of page. Never continue one paragraph from one page to the next. Be sure pages are numbered, and on the second and subsequent pages be sure they have all the info at the top that you have on the first page. If you have ever dealt with fax machines, you will understand why I say that. Pages get lost, get out of order, some are missing. Murphy's Law is truly in action.
- Before you send the release, make absolutely sure the facts are correct and there are no misspelled words. That is an indication of sloppy work. Let at least one other person proofread before you send it.

- At the bottom or the top, in a very prominent location type, "For more info, contact XXXX at (phone number)."
- There is nothing wrong with mailing a release to the media. But this is the 1990s, and you are much better off to fax the release or deliver it ASAP in person or by messenger.
- Not everybody agrees with this philosophy, but I have been very successful in what I call "papering the world" with a news release. It should go to the key person at all the media outlets. You should have determined these before you started your campaign. Your media list should contain the names of the key people, their addresses, phone numbers and fax numbers. I believe you make a big mistake if you start going through the media list and saying, "Naw, let's not send it to this person or that person." In every town, city, county, state, there are newspapers, radio stations, TV stations, cable outlets, etc., that cover the area where your voters live. I'm telling you from experience, you never know who will do a story based on your news release.
- At the end of the release, type "...end...."

When Should a Candidate Send Releases?

Whenever you have news.

Is It News? What Is News?

Is it out of the ordinary?
Is it timely?
Is it significant?
Does it have local appeal?
Is it emotional?
Does it have general interest?
Is there any element of conflict?
Will it jolt the reader or listener?
Did it happen locally?
Does it mention other names?
Is it what people are talking about?

When it comes to news, what one editor would consider news, another couldn't care less about.

I was flabbergasted as I traveled from town to town, county to county, to 627 towns in the state of Kansas. I did receive good coverage from a number of papers, but much to my surprise, a large number of the papers couldn't have cared less about me or my campaign. I truly was not looking for exceptional coverage just because I was in their town. But my campaign for Governor was the most extensive grass-roots campaign in the history of Kansas, and I may have been the first candidate for Governor ever to visit their town. And, to my way of thinking, that is news. Unfortunately, I was considered a non-news story in far too many towns for me to feel very comfortable about the small town news media in general.

One time I asked a reporter just what he considered to be news. He said, "The story must have in it something that is either new, surprising, creative or significant, or of special local interest." In the media we like "quotes," and if you can find a "first," then you have a story.

Four (pretty close to) Guaranteed Newsmakers:

1. Polls
2. Pictures
3. Mistakes
4. Attacks

Some Examples of Releases:

- ❖ When you announce that you are going to be a candidate
- ❖ The names of the people on your steering committee
- ❖ Endorsements of organizations and individuals you have received
- ❖ Your schedule for the week
- ❖ Your fund-raiser coming up at XXXX
- ❖ The invitation you received to talk at XXXX
- ❖ Announcing your stand on one issue at a time
- ❖ Your thoughts about a hot issue
- ❖ Sidebar story about one of your volunteers

Favoritism

It is not a good idea at all to play favorites when it comes to the media. You might make some great friends at one paper or station and seriously damage your reputation at another.

Yes, a paper, a station, a magazine may ask for an exclusive interview. That's okay. But when you have news of your campaign that you originate, tell everybody, and tell them all at the same time. Some of the media will use the information, some will not, but nobody will get uptight because you didn't play straight.

If you are dealing with only the weekly paper in your town, you can send them a release and title it: Special to the (name of the paper).

Fax Machines

There are fax machines on the market now into which you can program a number of fax numbers. When you have a fax to send, you merely put the fax in the machine, and it is automatically sent to all the numbers you desire—a great timesaver.

Best Time to Send Releases

The best times are on slow news days like Sunday and late at night or on a holiday.

Video News Conference

Some big-time corporations and public relations agencies record on video tape the basic information you would find in a news release, except it has moving pictures and action. They deliver this video either on a cassette or via satellite to television stations. Not a bad idea, but their effectiveness vs. their cost is a big question mark.

Guest Columns

Some candidates write a guest column on a subject of interest and submit it to their local editor. The chances of them publishing your column is surprisingly good. It is possibly a chance to get some good publicity. Try it.

Newspaper Clipping Service

Larger city campaigns and statewide campaigns would do well to have a clipping service clipping all articles about the candidate and the opposition. You can compare how much and how well you feel you are being treated by the paper vs. your competition. Unfortunately, you will not get the clippings for a week or more after they are published.

News Stories Vs. Newspaper Endorsement

It is nice to get the endorsement of the local newspaper, but many believe it is more important to get plenty of news coverage in the paper about your campaign. Campaign stories frequently are front page news, while endorsements are on the editorial page that many people never see.

Fighting with the Press

As the old expression goes, "Never fight with anybody who buys ink by the barrel." You're not going to always like everything that is printed about you. If you truly feel you have been unjustly dealt with, I suggest you sit down and "neighbor" with the editor.

Who Should Do Your Publicity?

Obviously someone who has some background in writing, someone who has some media contacts or has had experience dealing with the media. And a person who can help create a good image for the candidate and at the same time sell the candidate's program. The very best person and the person who can most influence how much publicity the candidate gets is, ultimately, the candidate.

Tips on Working with the Media

Become familiar with the names of the various newspapers, radio stations, TV stations and their editors, publishers, owners, their anchors and reporters. Then get to know these people in person. Call them and ask when it would be a convenient time for you to stop by and say hello. You won't develop these friendships overnight, but you need to work at it. Develop strong contacts; it will pay huge dividends.

Make sure you pronounce your contacts' names correctly and that you spell their names right.

As a candidate, make yourself accessible to the media. Some people hide from the media. I assure you that if the media is going to do a story that involves you, they are going to write that story with or without you. If you avoid them, you miss a chance to give the reporter your side of the issue.

I'm sure you have heard many times that the media is your enemy. That is nonsense. They have a job to do, and there are all kinds of reporters and editors. Keep your powder dry, deal with them honestly and straight, and you should have very few problems with them as I have over the years.

When you get a call from a reporter, editor, etc., return that call promptly. These people work on deadlines, so when you get a call from a member of the media, many times it means they need some information from you ASAP.

Never lie to a reporter. They have other sources than just you. They talk to many people, and if they find out that you weren't straight with them, you have ruined your credibility with them.

It is flat out not a good idea to talk to reporters off the record. I don't care if it is off the record or not, it is not smart to tell anything to a reporter that you wouldn't want to see on the front

Get Exposure/Advertising/Publicity

page of the newspaper or on the 6 p.m. news. I meet with a number of reporters and editors on a regular basis and talk freely, because I don't feel that I have anything to hide. They appreciate the honesty.

Don't tell a reporter, "No comment," when you are asked cold about something. It immediately gives the reporter, and the people who read the story, the idea that you have something to hide. About the best answer I have found for this type of situation is to say to the reporter something like this, "I'm working on that; I don't have anything now, but I expect to have a statement as soon as I can gather up more of the facts."

Don't discuss other candidates. Let them talk for themselves.

News people always appreciate possible story ideas.

The producers of radio and TV shows are always looking for guests for their shows. Get to know and stay in touch with these people.

When answering a reporter's question on radio or TV, think before opening your mouth, and make it short. Remember you are talking in sound bites. Your answers need to be short and concise. In responding to a newspaper reporter, talk slowly and thoughtfully. The reporter can only makes notes so fast. If you have something to say that is meaningful, say it slowly so the reporter can get every word of it correctly.

Ask your media contacts what information would be of value and interest to them that you could possibly provide.

Provide advance copies of your major speeches to the media, especially if they deal with controversial issues, or issues in which you know the media will be interested.

Never forget, the media loves controversy. Many a campaign has focused on controversies. It is a great way to keep the interest going in your local paper.

Write news releases on all your appearances. Write news releases on anything you do or say that would be considered news. You never know what places you are going to visit, or what activity you are going to be involved in, or what you will say that the media will want to cover. You should send your schedule at least three or four days in advance, even more if the paper has an early deadline. For radio and TV, talk to the news director about how much lead time would be preferable.

If you are going to call a news conference, do so after thinking about it. It should be a big deal before the media will have enough interest to cover it. If it relates to a juicy campaign issue, hold it someplace where the TV people can get good visuals and the newspaper photographer can get a great photo. Be creative.

Be sure that all media have one of your press kits. In addition to a good, professionally taken photo, either 5" x 7" or 8" x 10", you need to have a bio, campaign literature, copies of your news releases, issue papers, names of your steering committee members, etc.

Never tie the use of your publicity release to the placement of advertising. To say, "Give me some good publicity, and I will put a big ad in your paper," is an absolute no-no, and a dumb statement.

It is not a bad idea to get to know as many people at a newspaper and the other media as possible. You never know how a story idea may develop out of the blue that would mean added publicity for you.

Parroting

It is a common practice in political elections to find out what people want and need and what they are thinking. Then you need to say back to them exactly what they are thinking and how what you are advocating agrees with them.

Your Position on the Issues

Do your homework. Be sure your positions on the issues have been thoroughly thought out, and you tell the same thing to each group and to each reporter you talk to. Whatever you do, don't "wing" it; you will look like a fool.

Editorial Endorsements

Many newspapers have a policy of sending you a form to fill out outlining your stands on the various issues and your plans should you be elected. Sometimes these editorial endorsements are made based on these filled-out forms. Sometimes, depending on the office sought and the policy of the paper, endorsements are determined after a face-to-face interview with the editor or the editorial board.

Endorsements are nice to have, but don't think that once you get the endorsement of the local paper that you are a shoo-in.

Filling Out Surveys from Groups and Organizations

In larger elections you will receive forms to fill out indicating your positions on a variety of subjects "so they can inform their members." The letter accompanying the survey will indicate that this group has XXXX voters ("and they all vote"), who want to know how you as a candidate feel about this or that (usually controversial subjects like abortion, gun control, outcome-based education, etc.)

If you have the time and a staff and a desire, you may want to fill these out and send them in. I found out recently in a Governor's race that it was nearly impossible to fill out more than just a few of these surveys, because each one is usually five or six pages of questions. I made a determination as to those I felt were the most critical to my election and filled them out. If the survey was from a legitimate media source, I would fill it out. To the rest, I merely returned the survey with an info packet of my stands on issues and a bio with a note that said, "Due to a lack of staff and campaign pressures, I didn't have time, but I hope this information will answer your questions."

Obviously, if an organization had contributed to my campaign, I would have somehow been able to find time to fully answer their questionnaire.

Press Kits

Every campaign needs a basic press kit. You can buy the folder at a supply store, stick your campaign sticker on the front, fill it with your bio, candidate fact sheet, campaign photo, bumper sticker, position paper on your stands on issues and your latest news release, and you have a press kit. Every news director in your area should have one as soon as the campaign starts.

It should be neat, clean and professional looking.

Also, keep extras on hand. You will find that your original press kit was thrown away or can't be found by a new reporter. Be prepared.

Newspapers (General Information)

Inquire about local zoned editions of the metro newspaper covering your area.

Some candidates find that brightly colored flyers inserted in the local papers covering their area are very effective.

Make your newspaper ad headline a real "grabber." Many people read only the headline!

Some candidates write a weekly column for a paper and pay for it themselves.

Copies of your newspaper ads can be used in mailings to supporters.

Newspaper ads, where available in color, have a higher readership and a higher cost.

Smaller daily papers and weekly papers are often happy to accept articles from a candidate for publication.

Should You Hire an Advertising Agency?

That decision should be made only after you have an idea of what kinds of services you will need and if they can provide things that you can't take care of yourself. The size of your campaign will be the first factor to consider. In a small race, it is unlikely that any advertising agency would want to fool with you. Advertising agencies come in all sizes, shapes and descriptions. They provide a wide range of services, many specialize in a particular area of expertise. And most of them aren't going to cost you any more for their services than if you handled them yourself. They don't work for free. (After all, it's like a guy told me years ago, when you get something for "free," you really didn't get it free, you just haven't received the bill for it yet.) But they receive a commission from the media, art studios, printers and, as a result, you don't pay them anything extra for many of their services. They are set up to do such things as write ads, plan where best to advertise, lay out printed material, etc. You need to sit down with the advertising professional on your steering committee and make a decision after you check around and ask a lot of questions. If you decide to hire an agency, find one that has some past experience in working with a candidate for public office, and one that you feel very comfortable with. (Many advertising agencies want nothing to do with handling candidates running for public office.)

Whether you hire an advertising agency or not, the ads need to be prepared in conjunction with an advertising professional who is familiar with political advertising. This advertising has to have a lot of "sell" in it. As we used to say in the advertising business, there has to be more in the ad than pretty pictures and palm trees waving in the wind.

In political campaigns, you have to reserve space and time in advance. The best way is to plan your schedules working backward from election day, depending on your budget. You generally don't have to pay for the ads until 72 hours before they run, and you will have to pay for them CIA (cash in advance). That is standard for all political ads.

Radio (General Information)

When making a radio commercial, besides making sure it tells your story clearly, also make sure it is understood. I can't tell you the number of advertisers who have commercials that are read by a person who is difficult to understand. To me, it is another case of creative advertising. It wins awards but doesn't sell product. And as a candidate, you have a product to sell. That's you!

Television (General Information)

I believe TV commercials are most effective around newscasts and news shows.

Some campaign commercials lend gravity to the lightweight and importance to the insignificant. By inflating small facts, you can make a minor situation into a major event.

Research indicates that the best ways to draw attention to your ad is to use loud noise and sudden movement of light. This will immediately cause your attention to be focused on the screen and the commercial.

TV spots produced at locations that emphasize the issues of the campaign add credibility. An ad discussing senior citizen issues should be produced at a local retirement home or in the home of a retired local citizen, etc.

Almost all TV spots are either 10, 15, 30, 60, 90 or 120 seconds long (30s are the most common).

After all is said and done, to have an effective TV commercial: keep the message simple, use lots of good visuals, repeat your name verbally and on the screen, and ask for their vote. You can't discuss and solve all the problems of your area in a 30-second spot. (Somebody once said that the reason they are called "spots" is that TV is such a dog-eat-dog business.)

If you do an interview on TV, look at the person who is interviewing you and **not** at the camera.

A political guru once said regarding TV, "It's image that sells. The substance ain't worth a damn out there."

Billboards/Outdoor Advertising (General Information)

Boards come in various sizes, costs and formats. Their greatest advantage is that they are used to build quick name identification among the voters.

Your name should be in the largest letters on the sign. The fewer words on the sign, the more readable it is.

Lighted boards are worth the extra cost. Many people either drive to or from work when it is still dark.

You have to contract for boards months in advance, so if you are interested and they are part of your overall advertising strategy, you must make arrangements early. If you are offered some boards to rent, make sure you "drive" them. That is, travel the roads they are on to see how visible the sign locations are.

As with all advertising, the help of the advertising professional on your steering committee is invaluable (and if their expertise is not necessarily in billboards, they would know another professional who can help).

Vertical Media

Much advertising in vertical publications (specialty publications) can reach too narrow a group of voters and be of questionable value. But "for political reasons," ads are placed in circus programs, church bulletins, union newspapers, etc. They are generally way overpriced in comparison to ads in mass media. If you use them, tie your small ad to your affiliation with the organization, "Your fellow member, Jimmy Jones, candidate for XXXX would appreciate your vote on November 12."

If you are a member of a church congregation, a small ad in the church bulletin might be very beneficial in helping spread your name.

Campaign Literature/Brochures (General Information)

Years ago I saw a comment about literature in a campaign. I wrote it down and have tried not to forget it because it sums up the situation perfectly. "In the ideal campaign piece, the name is big, the pictures are many, the message is short, the issues are few. The campaign theme is bold, the colors are bright, the unity with other campaign advertising is dramatic, the language is simple, the white space is ample, and the appearance is inexpensive." I don't know who wrote that, but it says it all.

Early on in a campaign, your steering committee member in charge of literature production needs to determine the literature need of the campaign and get ready with the layout of the campaign literature in conjunction with your advertising strategy. There are all kinds of literature that will be needed, depending on how big your election effort really is. It is not unusual to have several mailers (that can also do double duty as handouts at meetings). You'll also need yard signs, stickers, buttons, reprints of favorable news coverage, copies of newspaper endorsements, papers on issues, sample ballots, etc. This is a big and extremely important job on the steering committee.

Each piece of literature should have a specific purpose. It should deal with issues or concerns or problems. A mailing that would go exclusively to senior citizens would deal with senior citizen issues. A mailing to parents with young children would deal with schools.

Whatever you do in the preparation of literature, use large type, plenty of pictures, have a short, meaningful, strong headline (most people will read only the headline), don't get too wordy, and have your name in big bold letters on both sides of the flyer (leaflet), mailer or brochure.

Realistically figure out how many pieces to print. You don't need a 20-year supply. But at the same time you need to anticipate your needs throughout the campaign, because you will run out of printed material. Make sure this doesn't happen by anticipating your needs and realizing that when many printers absolutely promise that the job will be done in one week, you know in your mind that the job will take at least two weeks. I've been fortunate—I have a friend who is also a printing jobber. He works with a number of printers and can get me printing in a big hurry if I need it.

Study old political brochures for ideas. Every politico I know has a folder full of them for that very purpose.

Be sure all the graphics on all your literature, campaign material and advertising are coordinated. The same colors, the same theme, the same type styles, the same basic message, etc.

Some political campaign pros believe that if the emphasis of your mailer is telling the voter "what's in it for them," how they will personally benefit if you are elected, then you will have a good, effective mailer.

It is your campaign and the object is to win. So remember that sometimes the people who are designing your literature may know a lot about art and design, but are dumber than dirt about politics. That is why your steering committee member in charge needs to work closely with the designer and run the literature by the steering committee before it is printed for real world comments. In small campaigns, you might ask a design student or a design class at the local college to design some literature for you, for a small contribution to the college scholarship fund.

When sending a letter to voters or designing a mailer to send, pretend that you are talking to just that one person.

All campaign literature is useless unless it is printed and delivered to the voter **before** the person votes on election day.

Each piece of literature should be designed to do double duty as both a mailer and a handout piece. That means having a facing side with a postal indicia, a return address, and a place to stick a mailing label or write an address.

Good Words to Use in Campaign Brochures and Literature:

Realistic, believable, sensible, frank, good taste, likeable, experienced, interesting, committed.

Thoughts About Headlines for Literature

Many people read only the headlines, so you had better have a good one. Make it short, interesting, punchy and thought-provoking.

Use large, bold type that is very easy to read.

If you can, try to paint a word picture with the headline that the reader can agree with. If so, you may have won his or her vote.

Since most people read only the headline, be sure to include your name in the headline: "Diane Linver, a good person doing an outstanding job in the legislature."

Some Thoughts About Yard (Lawn) Signs

Your signs should have the same design characteristics as the rest of your campaign materials. Same colors, same type styles, same logo, etc.

Even if you are working on a tight budget and the signs have to be hand printed, they still need to be all the same. Have you ever driven through a town while on vacation when it is election time? You certainly get an impression of the candidate from his or her yard signs.

Use big, bold letters and make sure they are readable at a distance.

In some parts of the country it seems to be customary to even have the candidate's picture on the sign.

Collect names of people who are willing to have a sign in their yard as soon as the campaign starts. Get crews and put up the signs about ten days before the election. Do them all on one weekend; it makes a great impression for the voters to drive down the street and see your signs on hundreds of lawns.

There are companies who print signs, bumper stickers, buttons, all kinds of political campaign material and giveaways, etc., for candidates. One of the very best is Gill Studios in Lenexa, Kansas. Call them for a catalog at 913/888-4422.

Generally, signs along the right-of-way of streets and within a certain distance of polling places are illegal. You need to check with your local election office and city hall for possible ordinances and restrictions in your area.

Sure, many candidates for city offices still use their own painted or stenciled signs. Nothing wrong with that as long as they create a good impression of you.

I have helped put up a lot of signs in my years as a political junkie. I will offer you a couple of tips: get good sticks that you can hammer in the ground without breaking for putting up yard signs. Also, have a good stapler to attach the signs to the stick **after** it is in the ground. (Don't staple the sign on the stick and then hammer it in the ground.) Use a good hammer with a big head on it. There are signs available that you merely slip over a wire frame.

For bigger signs, the big painted wooden signs made of a sheet of plywood, you will need a posthole digger. Better still, rent a gasoline-powered posthole digger. It will save you a lot of backache, time and trouble.

Thoughts on Other Campaign Material

Posters plastered around town will get you some name recognition. If you use them, make sure that they are put up in such a fashion that they will not bring you negative criticism and negative name recognition. Check on local ordinances.

There are thousands of advertising specialties, gimmicks and giveaways from matchbooks to golf tees to emery boards. Some people hand out seedling trees. I handed out sunflower seeds all over Kansas. If you use a gimmick, make sure it has some relationship to the campaign.

Regarding campaign buttons, it's unlikely that people will wear them day after day. But at something like a big gathering or festival, if they are personally pinned on supporters who will wear them, they will generate name recognition for you even though when the event is over, the button may very well be stuck on the recipient's wall as a souvenir. Caution: don't just hand them out; you will find that many people will say thanks and just put it in their pocket.

Make sure your name, the office that you seek and the name of your party is prominently printed on any item you use (you may even need a disclaimer).

Door-to-Door Distribution of Literature

When volunteers deliver literature door to door, you must stress the importance of *not* leaving the literature in locations where it will be blown around the neighborhood or scattered around the hallways of apartment buildings. That is very irritating to many citizens, and you don't need people talking negatively about you or your campaign.

Disclaimers

There are many laws around the U.S.A. relating to the need for and the content of a "disclaimer" on all your advertising and campaign material. The disclaimers usually say something like, "Paid political ad, Jimmy Jones, treasurer." They are usually in fine print and state who is responsible for the ad. The laws regarding these disclaimers are all over the place. I suggest you contact your Secretary of State's office and your local election office for the correct disclaimer necessary in your area **before** you have anything printed or any commercials produced.

Planning a News Conference

Find a convenient place.

Talk to your local news editors and reporters about the best time to hold one.

Besides newspaper reporters, expect that there will be TV and radio reporters. Make sure you have plenty of electrical outlets for the TV equipment. Some will need these, some will not. Ask them what they will need.

Contact all the local media by phone a day or two before, tell them you are going to make a very important announcement at a news conference to be held at XXXX. Then about 12 hours prior to the time, fax a reminder notice to them.

Don't tell the reporters the details of the conference over the phone. If you do, there isn't much reason to show up.

Hold the conference at a place that has something to do with your announcement. (Example: If it is about health care, hold it at a nursing home.)

In a businesslike way, stand up, welcome everybody. Read a prepared statement, and say you will be happy to answer any questions at the conclusion. If you have an 800 number to accept phone contributions, make a big sign of the number and hang it on the podium. Also on the podium should be one of your campaign signs, and signs should be all over the wall behind you so they can't be missed on TV.

Prior to the conference, sit down with members of your steering committee and come up with every conceivable question a reporter might ask at the news conference. Figure out how you will answer them. As the Boy Scout motto says, "Be prepared."

Have copies of your statement to hand out to the reporters.

Expect to have one or two general questions before you conclude. Then usually the reporters will want to individually corner you and ask you some questions.

There is nothing wrong with having some soft drinks and coffee and rolls, etc., available for the participants.

Getting Extra Mileage from Your Media Coverage

Send a photocopy of a favorable article to prospective donors. If you were on TV or radio, describe briefly what was on the air. Don't assume that everybody reads, watches and listens to the same media or as intently as you do.

You Are a Candidate 24 Hours a Day

If you are going to be interested and smiling, you need to be that way 24 hours a day. I have seen some candidates who are all campaign when going door to door, but when they go to the grocery store or hardware store, they are sourpusses and unfriendly. You can't turn your interest in people and issues on and off like a faucet. That brands you as a phony.

Aggressively Seek Publicity Opportunities

If you are going to be a candidate, you need to be seen everywhere there is any possibility of news coverage. And also you will need to be at many functions where it is unlikely there will be any news coverage.

Let the word out that you are available, and you are willing to talk to any club, judge a baby contest, cut a ribbon, etc.

Stay in contact with the members of the news media.

Besides the campaign issues, be sure they see you as a human being. The fact that your hobby is XXXX, that at college you did XXXX, your Uncle Louie who raised you came over on the boat with nothing but the clothes on his back and $5, etc.

A survey you take is always newsworthy. (If it shows you in a bad light, obviously you would want to use discretion.)

Talk to your radio station about their interest and use of actualities. That is where you will record a statement, call the station and ask them if they would like a statement from you about the XXXX controversy, or your stand on a particular issue, and then play it for them over the phone for use in a newscast. A good electronics store has all the necessary equipment to do actualities.

Write favorable letters to the editor, and have your friends write favorable letters on a continuing basis to the paper. Many newspaper surveys show that letters to the editor have very high readership.

When I ran for Governor, I held my news conference announcing the most extensive grass-roots campaign in the history of the state at a large retirement village (because I had just retired), and following the conference, I walked with reporters and friends to our Old Town historic district for a lunch of delicious tacos at Panzons Restaurant. I had a huge front-page picture and story, and stories on radio all day.

During my campaign for Governor, I invited editors and reporters to spend the day riding with us as we campaigned from town to town. A number of them took us up on the offer. We had a great time and had some great feature stories as a result.

I can't emphasize the fact enough that if you want exposure, make yourself available. If you get a call from a reporter, call back promptly.

Use a little showmanship! Your campaign only lasts so long, and you have a lot of ground to cover and a lot of name recognition to achieve. Carefully consider all publicity possibilities when you schedule anything or commit to any activity.

When I was Mayor, my wife and I slept in a "house" constructed of boxes of trash bags on the front lawn of City Hall. We were selling the bags to raise funds to sponsor a youth baseball trip. We received tremendous media coverage and had a great time until a powerful thunderstorm hit in the middle of the night.

Be sure reporters are aware of your schedule. Include some details that might interest them in covering your activities, like unusual topics of your speech, towns, clubs, who will be in attendance, etc.

When you think about getting publicity, you need to think in terms of news pegs. That is, the unique angle to your story that the reporter can write about.

Always think in terms of multiplying your effectiveness. You can shake only so many hands a day, and you need to do plenty of that. But a good story in the paper, on radio or TV will reach thousands of your potential voters. And if you get coverage over and over, your name recognition will soar.

When you want publicity, you need to do something, make something happen, make waves, make some sparks. You'll get noticed and get some publicity.

Never Forget

In life, your achievements are not achievements to anyone but you, unless they are reported in the media. That makes them official and credible. You can do all kinds of good things, but unless you tell the media about them and they are reported, not many people will ever know about them.

Some Thoughts About Photos in the Campaign

Have some good, clear, glossy photos taken by a pro. Don't use that old high school photo back when you looked like Miss Junior Miss or back when you had hair.

Have a number taken of different action shots in informal settings.

You'll need mostly black and white, but some color, 5" x 7" or 8" x 10"s. Order enough so you will have one to put in all the press kits you will be handing out, as well as some extra for emergencies.

Have pictures taken with other prominent, well-thought-of elected officials. If you have members of your steering committee who are well known, have your picture taken with them doing things, not just posed, standing there like a couple of bumps on a log.

Have your picture taken talking with citizens, like college students, young married couples, a family and their teenagers in their living room, single parents and senior citizens.

Have pictures taken at sites around town that you may have some involvement with. On the new street that you wanted constructed when you were a member of the City Planning Commission or the City Council. The new business that you helped convince to move to your community, or the park that you pushed and promoted.

Many papers will prefer to take their own pictures to use.

Have a good family picture taken of everybody, including the cat and dog. It will come in handy a number of times in the campaign. Not every family picture is a positive as far as publicity is concerned. I can visualize a woman candidate in a picture with a baby or young children that might send the wrong signal to some people, such as, "She should be staying at home and caring for that baby rather than running around town trying to get votes." So, use discretion.

Talk to editors about the technical requirements that photos need to meet before being published. Different papers have different standards.

Thoughts About Advertising

You will find that everybody either considers himself an expert or has some very definite opinions about advertising.

The key to success of an advertising message is in the mind of the voter, **not** in the mind of the candidate. What people believe to be true is more important than what is, in fact, true.

Talk about what the voter is interested in, concerned about, not on what the candidate is interested or concerned about.

Advertising can't make people accept or believe what they are unwilling to accept or believe.

Some candidates find this offensive, but the truth is that you "sell" yourself and merchandise yourself in many of the same ways that Proctor & Gamble sells detergent.

The key to success in political advertising is repetition. You must repeat your message and your name over and over, and over and over and over....

The purpose of advertising is to inform, but also to arouse passions, stimulate emotions and polarize people on different sides of an issue.

Much advertising in a political campaign for local or state office will reach greater numbers of people and a greater area than you need to reach. When placing your paid advertising, carefully consider this.

All advertising is expensive or cheap, depending on how you use it. For a retail business, if it brings in customers and sales at a reasonable cost, it is cheap. If it doesn't it is expensive. The same is going to be true for a candidate. You should have the advice of an advertising professional in selecting what media to use, or you will be overwhelmed and confused. There are many ways to advertise. It will take plenty of study to determine what media is going to be best for your situation.

Before you talk to any salespeople from the various media, I highly suggest you get a list of all the media in your area (newspapers, radio, TV, cable and billboard companies). Sit down with this list and your advertising professional who is on your steering committee and talk about all the pluses and minuses of advertising in each of these media. There are pluses and minuses to advertising in every media. Remember, you are not Ford, or GM, or Honda. You can't just buy everything. On your budget, you have to be extremely selective, and you will have a difficult time doing it.

If you have some local successful retailers who are friends and who do a lot of advertising, I'd talk to them also. (I emphasize the word successful, because everybody has an opinion about where to advertise. What you need is not just opinion, but opinion based on factual experience from someone who has used advertising successfully.)

Get Exposure/Advertising/Publicity

The absolutely toughest job you will have in a campaign is making good use of your precious campaign funds. You will be bombarded by friends and salespeople to buy all kinds of things. And believe me—I was in the advertising business for more than 30 years—everybody has a convincing story about how what they are selling can turn your campaign into a winner. (That's what selling is all about.)

In truth, nobody knows what works and what won't work at any particular time. If it were so easy, you'd put all the info into a computer, push a few buttons, and the answer would come flying out at you. You have a campaign to run, you don't need to spend all your time trying to figure out the advertising. But you do need to get with people that you know who are knowledgeable about the overall advertising picture in your area and trust their judgment. Trying to figure it all out yourself will drive you bonkers.

Even people knowledgeable about advertising will have very different opinions. As an example, if you have a limited number of dollars to spend, you can put little ads in a bunch of papers or editions of the paper over a period of time, or you could spend it all, making a big splash with one or two half-page ads. It is the old dilemma of should we buy a little of everything or a lot of a few things. The shotgun or the rifle approach to advertising.

With ads, it is important that you place them from the day before election day back. You need to hit people and remind them to vote for you just before they go into the election booth. Your heavy advertising should be crammed into the few days before the election. I don't care what the opponent does. Let him or her spend the money (waste the money) as they wish. Your ads are more effective very close to election day, and that is when you need to really heavy-up. Be careful, and don't get nervous. It is a common campaign ploy for one candidate to start an advertising blitz a good month or more before the election on the idea that the opponent will say, "I had better run a bunch of ads to counter those the other side is running." All this is done hoping that you will blow a lot, if not all, of your precious funds on ads at the wrong time and not have any money left to run them at the right time, that is just before the election when they are the most effective. It is dumb to be caught out of gas when you really need to make an impression.

No one advertising media alone will get you elected. They all have their strengths and weaknesses. Every campaign does not need every form of advertising. You and your advertising advisors need to figure out how to maximize your efforts to reach all your voters.

Naturally, you want to be sure that what you do regarding advertising is in line with your campaign strategy.

It is absolutely necessary in advertising to have maximum effectiveness. You need to use the same theme, the same colors, the same type of graphics and type faces, the same logo in **all** your ads, brochures, flyers, bumper stickers, yard signs, etc. It is what some people call "2 plus 2 equals 5." When things are coordinated, they have a much greater overall effect.

After you have decided what stations and papers you plan to advertise in, book your time as soon as possible. Space and time do get filled up, and the sooner you book it, the better chances you have of getting the times and locations you want for your ads. It is first come, first served. You don't have to pay for the ads when you book the space or time, but you will have to pay for the ads with your good check about 72 hours before they start to run.

Get Exposure/Advertising/Publicity

Allow plenty of white space in your ads. Don't clutter them up.

I feel that most campaign brochures, flyers, mail-outs, letters, etc., are way too long and way too windy, and the type is way too small. Not everybody wears glasses, but older voters need to be able to easily read your brochure more than younger voters. They proportionately care more and vote more. I know that it may hurt you to hear me say this, but seriously, nobody gets up in the morning and says, "I can't wait for the mail because today I will get candidate Jones' campaign mailer." Nobody sits around waiting for an opportunity to read your literature.

In all your newspaper ads, include your campaign phone number.

When you write your ads, make sure they are simple and easy to understand and read. Stay away from "cute" graphics. Some graphics people think it is really neat to use all kinds of goofy type styles and graphics ideas. They usually have in the back of their mind winning some kind of design award. You don't need all that because you are trying to win an election, not a design award. The walls of advertising agencies all over the world are lined with awards for advertising designs of advertising campaigns that were failures. But the artwork and design was beautiful! And in your ads and commercials, stay away from all the "two-bit" words. You're not trying to impress anybody with how smart you are and all the big words you can use. You are talking to "Betty and Joe, average citizen-voter on 83rd Street," and that kind of stuff will turn them off.

Not every radio and TV station has the same policy on whether or not they will accept political ads, or when they can run, or in what kind of programs they can be aired. Very early on you need to gather this information from the sales manager of each station.

Ratings

In any discussion you and your advertising professional have about radio or TV advertising, you will talk about ratings. Ratings are audience estimates, and I emphasize the word *estimates*. While they may be from a statistically-correct survey of several hundred people, and they are a good indication, you don't want to bet the farm on them. It is not an exact science.

You can get an indication from ratings of the relative demographic audience. That is, by age categories, whether it be young adults 18-34, or senior citizens 50-plus, and what programs and stations they listen to and watch.

As a general rule, people click around and channel surf and watch various programs on different channels on TV, whereas on radio they tend to put their radio on one station and rarely change it.

Comparison Impact of the Various Advertising Media

I tried to learn a few things in my years in advertising sales and management. One thing that is a real truism is this. Most people have no idea where or when they saw a particular commercial or exactly what the commercial really said. They gather little pieces of it, but rarely does a person sit glued to the set watching and hanging on every word.

Many times over the years after I had contracted with a client for an advertising schedule advertising a particular item exclusively on our station, I would ask the client (usually a retail merchant) to ask his customers, as they came in, where they saw the client's advertising. After two or three weeks, looking at the retailer's tally sheet, you found that maybe only one customer out of four would name your station, even though it was the only place that the store and the particular item was advertised. The list of places named would include almost every radio, TV and cable station, as well as all the various newspapers. People really don't know where they have seen or heard your ad.

Controlled Communications

Maybe you can't always control what the article said about you in the paper, or what one of your campaign workers told a voter over the phone. But your literature, flyers, brochures, newspaper, radio and TV ads are yours to tell your story. You control them and you can tell your story the way you want it told. Carefully look over all material before it is printed or goes on the air.

Paid Ads and "Free" Ads ("Earned Media")

Paid advertising is just what it is. You pay for the ads, and you get what you paid for. The so-called "free" ads (or as some people call them, earned media) are not ads as such, but are name mentions, photos and stories that appear in the media about you and your campaign. They could be news stories, a picture of you talking to the local Rotary Club, your ideas vs. your opponent's regarding an issue, etc. How much "free" advertising you receive is primarily dependent on your publicity and public relations efforts.

Buying Time and Space

Buying advertising space in a newspaper or buying time on a radio or TV station for your ads (commercials) is a tricky and complicated business. If you think it is easy, you are in for the shock of your life.

Layout and Production of Ads

Newspaper ads need to be designed to grab attention and get your message across. Your radio ads need to take your message, repeat it several times in several different ways, and emphasize your name a number of times. Your TV ads need to use the elements of voice and motion and graphics to tell your story. The production (the putting together) of these ads so they are ready to go in the paper or on the air can be inexpensive or expensive, depending upon a number of factors. The advertising professional on your steering committee can help you find people who know what they are doing and can do a good job. I know you have all heard that it costs thousands and thousands of dollars to put together a TV commercial. In some instances that is true, but you will find that if you ask around, check a person's background, check the ads that the person has put together for other clients, compare prices, you can find an advertising person who can put together a good commercial for you at a very reasonable cost.

And the time to produce your ads (paper, radio, TV) is very early in the campaign, **not** three weeks before the election. Not only are you going to be needing all your energy to finish the campaign, but you won't be as fresh as you would be early on.

Comparative Advertising

Some people consider "comparative" advertising to be "negative" advertising. What is wrong with comparing yourself and what you advocate with the programs and what your opponent advocates? Nothing, as long as what you say is true and what you say is believable and seems fair.

If You Catch Your Opponent in a Lie

Call his or her hand. Don't mince words. Let the reporters know loud and clear that your opponent is lying. But be sure you can prove it.

Sound Bites

Strategists who run big-time campaigns use "sound bites" because they believe that most voters do not read or reason well enough or care enough to do even elementary political or economic analysis. That is why you need to keep your campaign message very simple and repeat it over and over.

Admitting Mistakes

Nobody's perfect. We all make mistakes. If you do, admit it, correct it, and move on. Period.

Don't let your big ego make you reluctant to admit you're not perfect. I saved a note that I wrote down years ago. I don't know the author, but it is right on. "In a democracy, hypocrisy is a mortal sin. Americans think of themselves as tolerant, just as long as mistakes are admitted and explained, but are *unforgiving* of those who hide their errors behind a wall of indignation."

Equal Time

Note: This comment only applies to radio and TV stations, not to newspapers or to cable stations.

In some instances, you need to check with your local radio and TV station regarding current policy. They will have a policy regarding equal time in some political situations. If your opponent is given free time, you need to ask for equal time. If your request is denied, try to capitalize on that by publicizing the rejection.

Anger

Whatever you do, maintain your cool with the people you meet or come in contact with. As you have heard me say before, not everybody will love you, and some people think it is cute to "rattle your cage." It is important to remain calm and composed, and don't show your anger. I know there are times when it will be difficult, but don't blow it. When you do, you make the opposition look good.

Letters to the Editor

There have been studies made that indicate that Letters to the Editor are among the most read part of a paper. It would help to have your steering committee members and other volunteers write to the editor on a weekly basis about how good a person you are, or how much you are needed at City Hall to clean up the mess, etc. It is not out of the ordinary to ask volunteers to write a short positive note on a particular subject on a particular day. With some sort of organized schedule, your letters will be spread out, the subjects varied, and from all kinds of different people.

"Talk Back" Opportunities in Newspapers/Radio/TV

Some newspapers have a "talk back" column where readers can call in and anonymously express their opinions about almost any topic. And a growing number of radio and TV stations also offer you the chance to give your opinions. Here again, these are great places for your volunteers to talk positively about you and your campaign.

The Other Person Talking About You

It is very difficult for a person to get up and essentially say, "I'm a wonderful human being, vote for me." That is why you need to have your supporters doing a lot of good positive talking about you, your character and involvement.

Talk Radio Shows

When a topic of interest comes up, call them. You can't be shy. It is a great way to get your name and your ideas into the conversation. And encourage your friends and volunteers to do likewise.

Endorsements

Editorial endorsements and endorsement ads featuring the names of a long list of supporters have their greatest influence on the undecided voters. And in any close race, the undecided voters are the ones who can swing an election to one candidate or the other.

Direct Mail

You may have a mailing to potential contributors. You may have a mailing of a campaign brochure to voters. They are both considered direct mail.

In one mailing, you mainly ask for money, but you also talk about the campaign. In the other, you talk about the campaign, but like all your literature, you also ask for money.

If it went through the mail to the voter, it is direct mail.

Some Thoughts on Printing

What you will be bid for printing jobs will vary widely. You need to have your printing jobs bid out by several printers before you give the go-ahead. The advertising professionals on your steering committee will help you in this regard. I highly suggest you check with other candidates in previous elections and get their opinions of printers and their work. Printing is a complicated business, and there are lots of tricks of the trade. You will find out that quality will vary and reliability will vary. Printing jobs most often take more time than the printer has estimated. So I caution you to get hot on your printing early in the campaign so you can have your mailings and literature out on time for distribution.

If you are from a "Union" area, be sure to have the printer include the union "bug" on your literature.

Speakers Bureau

In any campaign, you will have many more places to go and talk about your race than you could possibly make. Your friends, often the members of your steering committee, will volunteer to speak at these gatherings on your behalf. They would be familiar with you and the campaign so they could talk with authority about the issues and your positions.

Chapter 15

Volunteers and Campaign Workers

▼

***The Best Advice from
Congressman Sam Brownback of Kansas***

"Have fun, because if you're not having fun, neither are the people."

Some Thoughts:

Make sure you truly appreciate the efforts of your campaign workers. Show it and express it over and over. Saying "thank you" and "you're terrific" and meaning it are like magic.

Some campaigns have many volunteers, others have only a few. It is not that the candidate doesn't have supporters, there just isn't that much for volunteers to do. And the last thing you want is a situation where you have volunteers sitting around drinking coffee with nothing productive to do. If people are going to volunteer their valuable time to help you, you had better make it meaningful, or you may lose a supporter. Don't ask for or recruit volunteers unless they can do something meaningful in the headquarters or out of the headquarters.

Your volunteer chairperson on your steering committee is in charge of volunteers. That person has a huge, very responsible and key position in the campaign. He or she should have a long list of meaningful activities to be dealt with and be constantly adding to that list as the campaign goes on.

And he or she should be aware of the many sources of good volunteers in the community. Teachers (during the summer especially), retirees, students, many people who you remember from doing volunteer work for other organizations. Good people are available from all walks of life, but you have to ask them to help. There are many reasons that people volunteer, or would volunteer to help you, but none is more important than the fact that you asked them.

Generally Monday and Friday are **not** good days for volunteers.

Recognize your volunteers and make them feel important because they really are. A friend told me one day, "There is no easier way of binding a person to a cause than to get them to do a little work for you."

It is impressive to see volunteers going from door to door in your behalf, or handing out literature at gatherings or in front of the local supermarket. And your opponent will notice also. **But no one should work harder than the candidate.**

Don't be naive. There are people whose word is no good. They will promise to do something and not get it done, giving all kinds of excuses. Don't get excited, it happens in all campaigns.

Have refreshment at headquarters for your volunteers and occasionally order in some pizzas or sandwiches.

If your campaign is like most others, you *will* have personality conflicts amongst your volunteers.

Some candidates choose to run a campaign using a mailing service to prepare, stuff and deliver their literature to the post office and professional phone personnel to canvass the electorate. In this way, the campaign is more expensive, but fewer volunteers are needed.

Just Some of the Tasks that Volunteers Can Handle Are:

- Doing filing at headquarters
- Typing thank you notes and campaign letters
- Canvassing voters over the phone or door to door
- Handing out literature at gatherings, door to door, or at high volume stores
- Being a poll watcher on election day
- Making sure people are, in fact, getting the absentee voter ballots they have requested
- Selling campaign T-shirts
- Obtaining locations to put up campaign signs
- Putting up yard signs
- Writing and organizing letter-to-the-editor drives
- Running errands
- Driving people who need assistance to polls on election day
- Baby-sitting for mothers so they can vote (if I were politically correct, I'd have said, "provide child care" for mothers, but I'm not politically correct)

- ❖ Doing campaign research at library on past campaigns and on the opponent
- ❖ Analyzing voting patterns in the district
- ❖ Preparing registered voter lists for candidate to efficiently walk door to door
- ❖ Checking nominating petitions and sending the signers a thank you note
- ❖ Answering the phone and taking messages at campaign headquarters
- ❖ Arranging a campaign rally
- ❖ Arranging for a place to have the election night victory party
- ❖ Arranging for people to donate food and drink for the party
- ❖ Decorating the place for the party
- ❖ Delivering news releases to the media
- ❖ Recruiting more volunteers for the campaign, etc., etc.

Chapter 16

Debates/Forums

**The Best Advice from
Congressman James L. Oberstar of Minnesota**

"Good organization is the first prerequisite for electoral success. The most brilliantly conceived campaign can falter without meticulous planning and organization.

I have always tried to draw my ideas and inspiration from the people I serve. And I have always tried to stay in touch with the people from all walks of life, never limiting input, advice and access to one or another group.

Finally, I have tried never to lose sight of the values I learned growing up on Minnesota's Iron Range:

1. Faith in God
2. Strength in Family
3. Hope in Community
4. Dignity in Work
5. Public Service as a high calling
6. Personal integrity

These core values have guided my public service—from teacher to campaign to member of Congress."

As a candidate, you will be invited to participate in what is loosely called debates or forums. The format for these exchanges will vary widely. Some will be pretty formal, where each candidate will have a couple of minutes to give an opening statement. Then the moderator will ask a series of questions, one at a time, and each of the candidates will have a minute or so to answer each of them. The forum would conclude with each candidate given a couple of minutes for a pitch regarding their qualifications.

When I first ran for Mayor, my kitchen cabinet was very concerned that I would get up and talk too fast and the audience would miss what I had to say. The cornerstone of my campaign was a "five-point plan." My advisors cornered me before the debate and emphasized over and over that I had to slow down my speech that evening as I presented my five-point plan.

The debate started; I got up and began talking very slowly and deliberately, going from point one to point two to point three. Just as I started talking about the third point, the timekeeper said, "Time's up."

When I ran for Governor, there were eight candidates, and our forums all over the state were often hardly worth the effort. In some ways, they reminded me of a TV newscast trying to tell about a big news story with a short sound bite. There were too many issues, too many candidates, and too little time. And very often there were almost as many candidates as voters in attendance.

Some Thoughts About Forums/Debates

Early on in the campaign, you should have prepared a list of anticipated questions and then prepared answers. You will hear the same questions over and over. If you have done your homework previously, you should be okay.

You still need to rehearse. Have somebody ask the questions, be critical of your positions, try to get you flustered, because that will be the scene at the debate. And the audience is as interested in seeing you get flustered as they are in your answers.

It was reported that in the famous Nixon-Kennedy debates, that JFK memorized a long list of dates, places, names and general information, and regardless of the question asked by the moderator, he would pull up some of that data. It created the impression that he was not only well-informed on just about everything, but was working on solutions to a lot of problems.

The sponsor of the forum will always ask questions relating to their special interests. A school PTA, a Chamber of Commerce, the medical group, the neighborhood association will all be interested in hearing about what's in it for them. I don't say that in a nasty sense but, after all, we are always looking out for ourselves.

In a forum, you don't have much time, so you better make sure you put your best foot forward, take the offensive, and come up with short, concise answers that show the real you.

The challenger always has the most to gain from the debate. Not only do you have a good chance to get your points across to the audience present, but you often will receive news coverage.

You would do well to be sure you understand and agree to the rules of the debate. Since you are also a participant, make sure the sponsor understands that you don't want your opponent setting the rules. It isn't so much the details as it is ego-deflating when you find out that the sponsor consulted your opponent and not you when setting the event up in the first place. And we all have egos.

Don't agree to debate unless you are convinced that it is to your advantage to do so. If you feel that a debate format has been stacked against you, turn it down, unless the sponsor can prove otherwise. That may sound trivial, but you could end up looking like a fool if you aren't careful as to what debates or forums you agree to attend. Never forget you are in a campaign, and only *one* person wins, the rest lose.

Talk to the audience, not to the other candidates or the moderator.

You have very limited time, so you cannot reasonably cover many topics. You're better off to stick with one or two points, and lean on them heavily.

You should try to get your opponent on the defensive. If he says that you want to spend money like it is going out of style, you then ask him what specific services he wants to cut? Close the swimming pool, do less street repair?

An old-time politico told me one time that debates were not for comparing and contrasting the positions of the candidates. They were hopefully an opportunity for a candidate to spring a devastating line on his opponent that will be positively reported in the news.

People go to debates, watch them on TV or listen to them on the radio, but not so much to learn about the issues. They watch them for the same reason most people watch the Indy 500—to see the crashes and burns.

Some Thoughts on Public Speaking

In any campaign, you will need a "stump" speech that you will give over and over, maybe a thousand times. It is the basis of your campaign. You will add some personalization to the beginning and name a few of the local people and something of local interest, but then you will deliver the rest of the speech from memory. You'll give it so many times, you'll be sick of hearing yourself, and your advisors will be sick of it, too. Leave it alone. Sure, there will be a few people who will hear the same speech you gave two months ago, but most of the voters will only hear you once and have never heard what you had to say until today.

Make your stump speech "you." Make it down to earth and emotional. Be sure it is well thought out and not too long and windy.

After speaking, maybe answer a question or two. But when you leave, you will invariably say to yourself that you stayed one question too long.

Never, never, never cover more than one or two main points in a stump speech. Support those points with ideas and stories, and call the people to action. Make it short, thank everybody, then sit down.

Use humor carefully. Not everybody can tell jokes or tell stories that have funny punch lines. If you can't, stay away from them. Every joke should have a point that has some connection to what you are talking about.

If you are going to tell stories, remember they have a beginning, a middle and an end.

The toughest part of writing a speech is getting started. You need to sit down, know the purpose of the speech, what ideas you want to get across, stories and ideas about them and background information. Use plain words, short, punchy sentences, and close with a strong statement or call to action.

Practice your speech. I have found that recording my talk into one of those hand-held mini-recorders works for me. I'll record, then listen and change some lines or phrases, then record over. I may do this eight or ten times before I get it the way I like. At that point, I make a clean copy of my speech, triple space it so I can read it without my glasses, take the recorder with me and listen to it a few times in the car on the way to give the talk. Take a deep breath, relax, smile, give the talk, be sincere, you'll do great.

Be familiar enough with your speech that you don't read it word for word.

If you're smart, you will write out your own introduction. I can't tell you how many times I have been introduced, and the emcee would leave out something that I felt was really important to me. You will find that the emcee would appreciate it if you would write out exactly how you want to be introduced.

Do not mention your opponent by name. That gives him or her free advertising.

Always ask for help—help in getting elected for sure. And **always ask for their vote!** Ask them to sign aboard and ride the train with you to the end of the line.

A woman candidate who wants to cut some of the flak she might receive might say in her remarks that she is "not a woman candidate. I am a Democrat or Republican candidate who happens also to be a woman."

In delivering the speech, you don't have to be the greatest orator in the world. Most times after I am introduced I tell the audience that it is great to have a chance to deliver my famous 45-minute speech. They know I am kidding. I get along very well by making my talks short and sweet, getting my points across and sitting down. I don't want to shock you, but nobody wants to hear a long-winded political speech.

Type your speech on 8-1/2" x 11" sheets and triple space. Start typing each page about a third of the way down. Take a felt tip pen and number the pages in the right-hand top corner. Don't staple them. If you don't number them, I'm telling you they will somehow get out of order.

Publicize your talks. A week or so before (not after, that's ancient history) you are scheduled to make any talk, send out news releases announcing that you are going to talk to XXXX group about XXXX at XXXX on XXXX. You will be delivering essentially your same stump speech over and over, week after week. When you send out the news releases, you have to be creative and remember that there are lots of ways in a release to say the same thing or deliver the same message and make it sound different.

Dale Carnegie said it best. When giving a speech, tell them what you're going to tell them. Tell them. And then tell them what you told them. And sit down.

Some "Plain" Words to Use in Your Talks/Speeches

hard work	family	home
love	land	dreams
growth	confidence	people
skills	feeling	thinking
change	commitment	learn
efficient	smart	positive

Get Elected, Make a Difference!

Nancy Becker, Dyan Conway Nichols, Kansas Governor Bill Graves, Rich

Chapter 17

GOTV—Get Out the Vote

**The Best Advice from
U.S. Senator Alan Simpson of Wyoming**

"If you don't know who you are before you get here, this is a very poor place to find out."

Having all kinds of endorsements, all kinds of friends and supporters, all kinds of good news from polls, all kinds of pats on the back and all kinds of good wishes aren't worth two hoots and a holler if you don't get your voters to the polls to vote.

Your GOTV effort will reflect how well you have your act together. Make sure that you:

Have a mailing or a last-minute door-to-door distribution of literature or a phone call to those who you have determined either favor or are leaning or are undecided. Be absolutely sure the voter knows the location of the polling place. Don't assume that he does, because locations do change. Obviously, don't encourage those who favor your opponent to vote. You're trying to win an election, not to be politically correct.

Have poll watchers stationed at the polls with lists of the registered voters to check off as people vote. The poll watcher's job is to check on *only* those voters you have been counting on, **not** the entire list of registered voters. At the polls, they may only watch what is going on, not make comments or editorial opinions, or the election judge may ask them to leave. They have to have credentials that are arranged through the local election office. He or she checks the counters on the voting machines to be sure they register zero, and to be sure that the ballot boxes are empty when the polls open. As the voter's name is called out, he or she notes it on their list. If the name and address is not on the list, the potential voter may be challenged in a businesslike manner. The election judge will have to make a ruling.

Ask volunteers to make calls from home in a smaller election to their friends as reminders.

Ask if people need a ride to the polls, someone to watch their children while they vote, or need some kind of special assistance. If they do, be sure you provide it.

Know where you can legally post signs, the distance you must be from a polling place to hand out literature, and the rules regarding wearing campaign buttons or material in a polling place, etc. There are all kinds of little things that can cause a ruckus. I remember when my kids were small, I took them to the polls with me and had a hassle with one of the election judges who said I couldn't take my kids in the voting booth with me. I lost!

Emphasize to your telephoners to remind people to vote, tell them where they vote, encourage them to vote for you, say thank you and hang up. Don't waste the voter's time with idle chitchat.

Use good old common sense in whatever you do, especially in the very hectic last days of a campaign.

Election Day Activities

Up to election day everything is preparation. Some people look at it like a one-day sale.

Your volunteers need to be trained as poll watchers to sit in polling places and check off voters as they cast their ballots. The poll watcher checks the sheet containing the list of names of people who have indicated a leaning toward your candidate. At about noon, phone calls and personal visits are made to get those people to the polls who have not shown up yet. Sometimes you need to provide transportation and baby-sitting for those wishing to vote. And this position also involves planning for the election night victory party along with the special projects person.

Get Elected, Make a Difference!

Kansas Delegation to the 1992 Republican National Convention in Houston

Chapter 18

Absentee Voters

**The Best Advice from
Congressman Sam Farr of California**

"My experience in local state and federal office has taught me that both the public and the elected officials have difficulty in getting to the point of an issue.

My advice to all:

1. Know what's broke that needs fixing.

2. After knowing #1, remember that 'the squeaky wheel gets the grease.' Petitioning the appropriate government does work, but you must work at it."

Don't overlook these voters. Some big-time elections, where one candidate thought he had won on election night, was disappointed to find that he was beaten once the absentee ballots were counted. Instead of spending your time getting people registered during the campaign, spend some time on a plan to get absentee voters to vote for you. It will pay much greater dividends.

Not everyone can or is able to make it to the polling place on election day. Each state has made provisions to allow people to vote who are going to be out of town on vacation, on business, away at school, in the military, sick at home, etc. Your Secretary of State's office will have the official rules and provisions. There are very definite rules regarding absentee ballot voting; make sure you understand them and follow them.

Across the country, state legislatures are making it easier to get absentee ballots and to vote in the days prior to actual election day in some situations.

As you go door to door or canvass over the phone, you will discover who may need an absentee ballot. Make the necessary arrangements for them to get one, and do it in plenty of time before the election so a ballot can be mailed to the voter, the voter can vote and mail it back by election day or the deadline set by the state.

Who can vote absentee will vary from place to place. Here again, you need to check with your Secretary of State to find out who is eligible. There are shut-ins, people in hospitals, people in the military, students going to a distant college, vacationers, and the business person who is just plain going to be out of town on election day.

Some states allow people to cast their vote a week or more prior to the election if they are going to be gone or just want to avoid the lines on election day.

Chapter 19

Legalities of a Campaign

▼

The Best Advice from
U.S. Senator Patty Murray of the State of Washington

"I would tell any candidate, no matter what advice you get, follow your own heart and soul, because it is you who will and only you who will live with how you present yourself for the rest of your life."

Your legal advisor on your steering committee will be up to date concerning current election laws regarding contribution limits, libel laws, filing dates, proper forms for filing nominating petitions. It really helps to have an attorney on your steering committee to give you some good free advice from time to time.

Election laws vary considerably from state to state, and many a candidate did not make it on the ballot or was knocked off the ballot at the last minute on a technicality. There are all sorts of rules and regulations that an attorney can interpret for you, from the need to get a permit to put up yard signs to the fine points of campaign finance reporting laws, to the deadlines for filing petitions.

Libel and Slander

Libel deals with what you write. Slander deals with what you say. In every campaign, there are some hot moments when occasionally things are written and said about the opponent that might be considered "reckless." That sort of thing can bring on a lawsuit.

Chapter 20

Civics 101 Vs. the Real World

▼

The Best Advice from
Congressman Benjamin L. Cardin of Maryland

"The best advice I can give is to be committed to improving the community, to establish rapport with neighborhood and community groups, and to understand and work with the political power structure of your state or community. However, the most important information I can give is to have well thought-out and creative proposals that improve life for others in your state or community."

Some Thoughts

When I was a kid growing up in St. Louis, my parents loved trees and flowers and nature in general. As a Boy Scout, I could name just about every kind of tree that grew in Missouri. I thought everybody loved trees. Years later, when I was Mayor, I found out to my surprise that there are many people who hate trees for a variety of reasons. They have leaves, the leaves fall in the fall, and they shade things in the winter, and that keeps the snow from melting. They block the view of a person's sign or business. And there are architects who only want to build square buildings and straight sidewalks because they are not creative enough to build around the trees. They want to strip the land bare, build a square building in the middle of the lot, and plant trees the size of your finger to replace the 100-year-old trees that they cut. In the real world, and in a growing city, it is not realistic to believe you can save every tree when doing construction. But we need to make sure we save as many as we can to preserve the beauty and benefits they provide.

The reason I bring up this subject is that different things concern different people, and when you are campaigning, you need to talk to people in terms of what *they* are interested in and concerned about.

Citizen Legislature

It sounds wonderful to say we have a "citizen legislature" making our laws. The truth is that only certain people can serve; many are excluded. In Kansas, for example, the legislature meets from mid-January through mid-April at the state capitol. How many businesses do you know of, or occupations that you can think of, that would allow you to take off for three months to do your duty as a legislator? I don't have the answer, but I'm working on it.

Citizen Activist...A Great Study of People

I first became active in politics as an activist. I remember years ago, before I was involved with city affairs, when shopping centers were being proposed on three of the four corners of a major intersection that kids crossed (including our own) to go to elementary school. I took out my felt tip pen and designed a flyer outlining the problem and asked citizens to come to City Hall for a meeting that was going to be held a couple of days later. I took the sheet to a quick printer and had a bunch of them printed. I took off work the next day and spent the whole day enthusiastically going from door to door delivering that flyer. I was fired up. When I got home at dark, as I walked in the door, my wife Nancy said that a lady had called and wanted me to call her back. I remember saying to Nancy that this is democracy in action. It's great, because I'm sure that this lady is concerned about the issue as I am. I called her, and as soon as I told her my name, she said, "You spelled the name of the street wrong!" She didn't care about the issue at all—she was more interested in saying "Gotcha!"

By the way, we had about 75 people at the meeting and the matter was resolved.

Your Duty as a Citizen

It is your duty as a citizen to stay somewhat informed about what is going on in the world around you, if for no other reason than to protect your interests. It is unrealistic to think that you, as a citizen, should concern yourself with every fine detail of city or state or federal government. It is impossible to keep up with everything. It has been my experience that people who are involved and care about a particular facet of government are really involved and really do care. But the truth is that the average citizen isn't as dedicated—that is, until the trucks show up on the lot across the street from their house and start digging the hole for the new Burger King that they "didn't know anything about"—on the lot that the real estate person said was going to be a park where their kids could safely play.

Chapter 21

Campaign Schedule

▼

***The Best Advice from
U.S. Senator Bill Frist of Tennessee***

"The best advice I received was from Congressman Jimmy Duncan (R-Tenn.). When I was considering running, I visited with Jimmy, and his advice was, 'Never pretend to be something you are not. It will always catch up with you. Be true to yourself.'"

When to Do What Needs to Get Done

There is so much to do and so little time once you start a campaign. One of the secrets is to really start your run for office before you "officially" start. That is, make the contacts, express interest, get reaction from possible supporters and contributors. An election for a state office may, in fact, start underground three or four years in advance. A run for Mayor of a medium-sized city may have an underground start a couple of years in advance.

Everybody's goal is to have his or her campaign peak on election day. Working toward that end, it is necessary to set up a schedule for your campaign so your goal is accomplished.

It is of interest that many pollsters believe that up to 20 percent of the voters don't make up their mind as to who they will vote for until they are in the voting booth. So publicity, advertising, mailings, personal contact and all the last-minute activities just before and even on election day could possibly sway some voters and be the margin of victory. In a recent election, I had one candidate call me an hour before the polls closed to ask for my vote in case I hadn't voted. (I already had).

If you have a primary election opponent, you need to win that election first. Here is a general outline of a schedule for a hypothetical June 15th *Primary:*

Prior to January 1

Enlist underground support for candidacy.

Line up key people willing to serve on your steering committee.

If you have some campaign seed money, commission a name recognition survey of your name vs. other leaders and elected officials in the area. Also take an issues survey to get some idea of what people are concerned about that you don't already know. The larger your campaign, the more detailed these surveys need to be.

Talk confidentially with party leaders, editors, news directors, your friends, family and business associates about your possible candidacy.

Research the library, your Secretary of State's office and Election Commissioner's office for past election results, financial contributors reports, filing information and election laws.

Analyze past voting patterns in your district.

Research your opponent's voting record and background.

Plan campaign strategy with your steering committee.

Work on ideas for your campaign literature. Have good campaign pictures taken, and put together all the basic elements for the media kit for the news media.

Decide on the issues you will talk about in the campaign.

Schedule to submit campaign financial reports as required to the proper state official on time.

January 1–March 15

Announce to the world publicly with much fanfare that you are a candidate. Make it a "big-deal" affair. Announce at a site that has some tie-in or news peg to what you are going to be talking about in your campaign. (If it is about roads, hold it in the middle of a street filled with potholes.)

Fill the slots of your steering committee with good, dedicated and committed people.

Recruit volunteers.

Put together a budget.

Locate a place to call "headquarters" and move in. Have phones installed, have stationery printed as soon as you have all your steering committee members in place so you can have their names prominently displayed on your letterhead.

With your steering committee, select a campaign manager.

Set up citizen committees like "Teachers for Serrone" or "Park College Alumni for Serrone."

Every week or so, announce with news releases the names—a few at a time—of the key people who are serving on your steering committee.

Your fund-raising efforts should be in full swing. The candidate will spend much time asking for money from those who could and should support him or her, while at the same time asking for votes. This will continue through election day.

Hold a major fund-raising event to scoop the opponent and possibly scare away some other potential candidates.

If you file by petition in your state or community, have volunteers collect at least double the number of signatures that are required.

Have your campaign literature printed, and have a good printer on standby in case you need a fast printing job done in the final days of the campaign.

Arrange for your advertising. Reserve ad space in the paper and on radio and TV if you have determined with your steering committee advertising professional that it would make sense to do so. (If billboards are in your ad plans, they need to be ordered months in advance. Check with your professional.)

Line up as many public appearances as possible through the week before the election. (Schedule appearances in the week before the election later when you have a much better idea of where you need to be spending your time in the crucial final week.)

Plan your strategy and be sure all your steering committee members are in sync.

Get publicity. Continue making talks to groups and going door to door. Keep the media informed of your activities.

Start soliciting locations to put up yard signs.

Ask friends and possible supporters to do volunteer work in the campaign.

March 15–April 15

Obtain current list of registered voters in your area. *Note:* In this primary election, only concern yourself with those voters who are eligible to vote in this primary election. Don't waste your time or energy or money on people who cannot vote in this election because they are of the other party or are registered as an independent (unaffiliated) voter. Double check the election laws in your state for the correct information.

In smaller campaigns the candidate will walk door to door canvassing the voters. In larger elections the candidate may do some door to door, but most of the canvassing of the registered voters who are able to vote is done over the phone. Sometimes the canvassing is done by volunteers going door to door, but more commonly these days it is done over the phone.

Solicit endorsements from leaders in the community and from clubs and organizations where possible.

Get publicity. Make things happen, make news.

Continue going door to door and making talks and meeting the voters.

April 15–May 15

You will officially file as a candidate by whatever method you have in your state and community—whether by petition or by paying a filing fee or whatever. Check the date of the filing deadline. And don't miss it!

Have mailings and literature sent to the registered voters who can vote in this primary election.

Visit with editors and news directors and solicit their endorsements.

Solicit names of friends and supporters to use in the big newspaper's endorsement ad just before the election.

Make sure you have arranged to have absentee ballots sent to all those who have requested them.

May 15–June 14

Have a mailing arrive about the 7th of June, and another to arrive the Saturday or Monday before election. (Be very careful to send these by first class mail, and even at that there is no guarantee they will be delivered when you hope. Many a candidate's mailings have arrived after the election, so be sure you mail in plenty of time.)

Start running your ads in the paper, on radio and TV. Schedule them from the day *before* the election backward. Concentrate on the few days prior to the election, depending on how much money you have.

About ten days before the election, preferably on a Saturday, put up your yard signs all over town.

On the day before the election, have your telephone volunteers call those who favor you and those who are undecided, to remind them to vote for you. Also, be sure to tell the location of their polling place. (Don't call or send literature to, or encourage those who have indicated that they favor or are leaning in favor of your opponent.)

A day or two before the election, place a large newspaper ad listing the names of many people in the community who endorse you.

Be prepared to counter an "eleventh-hour sneak attack" by your opponent. (In Lenexa we call these a green light special). They are the attacks on you, usually with a completely false statement, that are mailed or ads that are placed at the last minute before the election that are difficult to respond to because there isn't time. In this computer age and with quick print shops, it is amazing how fast you can get a piece of literature out to the voters either through the mail or hand delivered to counterattack if necessary.

June 15 (Election Day)

Very early on election day morning, make sure all your signs in the vicinity of the polling places are still up. In some campaigns, yard signs of one candidate or another tend to disappear or get knocked down.

Try to get election day coverage on the news early in the day.

Have poll watchers at the polls. Make calls to potential supporters to encourage them to vote.

Have one person assigned to each polling place to get the vote totals after the polls close and call them into your headquarters.

Plan a small victory party. Hopefully you will win. If you do, you now have a big-league race ahead. If you didn't win, be sure to call the winner and congratulate him or her.

Day *after* Election Day

Win or lose, send thank you notes to those who helped.

Win or lose, take down your yard signs.

Now we go on to the general election since you were victorious. Take a day or two and "get the heck out of Dodge" and relax and get away from all this politicking. When you come back, you'll need to be refreshed, because the main event is before you. You have a lot of work to do.

Be sure to spend your time efficiently and effectively, and always "fish where the fish are" or "hunt where the ducks are." Concentrate your efforts on the areas where canvassing shows you are the strongest, and try to get even more support, *rather than* concentrating where your opponent is strongest. (In my campaigns for mayor, there are several precincts that I never was able to win regardless of the opponent or the issues.)

If you *did not* have a primary election, you now face a general election on the first Tuesday in November.

Here Is a Schedule to Follow:

Prior to September 1

Enlist underground support for your candidacy.

Line up key people willing to serve on your steering committee.

If you have some campaign seed money, commission a name recognition survey of your name vs. other leaders and elected officials in the area. Also take an issues survey to get some idea of what people are concerned about that you don't already know. The larger your campaign, the more detailed these surveys need to be.

Talk confidentially with party leaders, editors, news directors, your friends, family and business associates about your possible candidacy.

Research the library, your Secretary of State's office and Election Commissioner's office for past election results, financial contributors reports, filing information and election laws.

Analyze past voting patterns in your district.

Research your opponent's voting record and background.

Plan campaign strategy with your steering committee.

Work on ideas for your campaign literature. Have good campaign pictures taken, and put together all the basic elements for the media kit for the news media.

Decide on the issues you will talk about in the campaign.

Plan campaign strategy with your steering committee.

Locate a place to call "headquarters" and move in. Have phones installed, have stationery printed as soon as you have all your steering committee members in place so you can have their names prominently displayed on your letterhead.

Schedule to submit campaign financial reports as required to the proper state official on time.

September 1–September 15

Traditionally, November election campaigns begin on Labor Day.

Announce to the world publicly and officially with much fanfare that you are a candidate. Make it a big affair, but don't do *it* on Labor Day. Pick a day when you can get the most publicity. Check with the editor and news directors. Announce at a site that has some tie-in or news peg to what you are going to be talking about in your campaign. (If it is about crime and jails, hold it outside a prison.)

Fill the slots of your steering committee with good, dedicated and committed people.

Put together a budget.

With your steering committee, select a campaign manager.

Every week or so, announce with news releases to the media the names of the key campaign people on your steering committee.

Your fund-raising efforts should be in full swing. The candidate will spend much time asking for money from those who could and should support him or her, while at the same time asking for votes. This will continue through election day.

Hold a major fund-raising event to scoop the opponent and possibly scare away some other potential candidates.

If you file by petition in your state or community, have volunteers collect at least double the number of signatures that are required.

Arrange for your advertising space and time. Reserve ad space in the paper and on radio and TV if you have determined with your steering committee advertising professional that it would make sense to do so. (If you are going to use any billboards, they usually have to be booked months in advance.)

Line up as many public appearances as possible until the week prior to the election. (You can schedule your appearances for the final week later after you have a better idea of where you really need to be campaigning in that crucial period of time.)

Plan your strategy and be sure all your steering committee members are in sync.

Make sure your volunteer activities are coordinated. If you are going to ask your volunteers to be at headquarters on a certain date and time to help with a big mailing, make sure that you have your act together and **all the necessary materials** are ready. You'll lose your volunteers fast if they feel that you are disorganized. They will praise you if they find that you are really on the ball and everything is ready for them to immediately go to work.

Get publicity. Continue making talks to groups and going door to door. Keep the media informed of your activities.

Make sure all campaign material is printed and ready to go. And have a good printer in mind if you need a fast printing job done in the hectic days just prior to the election.

Obtain a current list of registered voters in your area. Since this is a general election, all voters of all parties, as well as anyone registered as independent or unaffiliated can potentially vote for you.

September 15–October 1

You will officially file as a candidate by whatever method you have in your state or community—whether by petition or by paying a filing fee or whatever. Check the date of the filing deadline and don't miss it.

Analyze voting patterns. Pay particular attention to historical voters.

Start canvassing the registered voters. You need to find out if they are for you, leaning toward you, undecided, leaning toward your opponent, or are for your opponent. In smaller campaigns the candidate can often determine this by going door to door of registered voters. In larger campaigns this canvassing is usually done over the phone by volunteers making calls from headquarters, or by hiring a professional phone service.

Solicit endorsements from leaders in the community and from clubs and organizations where possible.

Set up citizen committees, like "Teachers for Klein" or "Tiffiny College Alumni for Klein."

Get publicity. Make things happen, make news.

Continue going door to door, making appearances, meeting the voters and asking for their vote. And keep raising money.

October 1–October 20

Have mailings and literature drops to the registered voters. (Eliminate from your mailing list those who have indicated in canvassing that they favor the opponent.)

Visit editors and news directors and solicit their endorsements.

Solicit names of friends and supporters to use in the big newspaper ad just before the election.

October 20 Till Day Before Election Day

Continue your appearances and contact with the registered voters. Every possible moment should be spent as efficiently as possible in voter contact.

Make sure you have arranged for absentee ballots for anybody who might need one.

Keep up your publicity. Do things, make news, keep the media informed of your activities.

Campaign Schedule

Have a mailing arrive at the homes of registered voters about ten days prior to the election, and another to arrive on the Saturday or Monday just prior to the election. (Send by first class mail, and be sure to mail in plenty of time and hope they arrive when you have planned.)

Start running your ads in the newspaper, on radio and TV. Schedule them from the day *before* election day backward. Concentrate on the few days prior to the election, depending on how much money you have.

Maybe plan a rally the day or two before election day.

About ten days before the election, preferably on a Saturday, put up yard signs all over town.

On the day before the election, have your telephone volunteers call those who favor you and those who are undecided and remind them to vote for you. Also be sure to tell them the location of their polling place.

A day or two before the election, place a large newspaper ad listing the names of many people in the community who endorse you.

Arrange for baby-sitting for mothers so they may vote, and transportation for elderly who need it.

Be prepared for any last-minute attacks by your opponent. You may be able to send a special mailing to counter his or her charges.

Election Day

Very early on election day, have your volunteers check to be sure that your signs in the vicinity of the polling places are still up and in good condition.

Try to get election day coverage on the news, early in the day.

Have poll watchers at the polls. Make calls to potential supporters encouraging them to vote.

Have one volunteer assigned to each polling place to get the vote totals after the polling place is closed, and call them in to your headquarters.

Have a victory party. Thank everyone for their efforts.

If you won, Congratulations. Graciously accept the congratulations from your opponent.

If you lost, call your opponent and offer congratulations. I know it is tough, but it is the right thing to do. And you always want to do the "right" thing.

Day *After* Election Day

Win or lose, send thank you notes to all those who helped.

Keep your election records, like lists of supporters, canvassing records, locations of yard signs, etc. You will want to refer to them at next election time. Don't let them get away.

Win or lose, take down your yard signs.

For your personal benefit, sit down in a quiet place, reflect on the campaign, what you learned, what was good and what was horrible. Write down your thoughts about any and everything, not for the public or anyone else to see, but just for you. So you can refer back to it someday, long after the wounds have healed and you have moved on to bigger and better things, either as the victor or as the person who "almost won." I have notes of past elections, but not as extensive as I wish I had kept. Running for office is one great experience!

Note: While these schedules will give you a pretty good ballpark idea of how things should fall in order, they should only be used as a guide. Every campaign is different. From these guidelines, you will want to lay out a much more detailed schedule of very specific things that need to be accomplished and a time frame (firm) for getting them done.

A campaign among candidates can vary from one extreme to the other. And they are different from an issues campaign, like a ballot proposition to have the community build a new school or jail. Above all, let good old common sense prevail. And remember, you get involved in these campaigns to *win,* not to have a good feeling or to make friends or whatever. If you are going to get involved, don't let any stone go unturned in your quest to win.

When the election is over, win or lose, you want to be able to say to yourself that you did everything you could possibly have done with the time, energy and money you had. You have nothing to be ashamed of, and if you won, you are now in a position to change things and make a difference. If you lost, you can hold your head up high and be very proud that you did the best you could possibly have done. Don't waste a minute second-guessing yourself, get on with your life.

Get Elected, Make a Difference!

The Best Advice from
U.S. Senator Carol Moseley-Braun of Illinois

"I believe in the importance of citizenship. Every person has a duty to try and make our country a better place. I ran for office because my son worried that my generation was going to leave the country in worse shape than it found it. I thought I could help change that as a United States Senator of Illinois.

Every time a person votes, or runs for office, or participates in the political process in any way, they are contributing to our democracy."

"If you don't run, you can't win!" —Rich Becker

Chapter 22

Wisdom, Thoughts, Truisms and Quotes

***The Best Advice from
Congressman Harry A. Waxman of California***

"Sam Rayburn often said that 'Politics is the most honorable profession in the world. A man could have no higher ambition than to get in a position to serve other people. Service is the greatest word in the language.'

I have often thought of Speaker Rayburn's quote when Congress is ridiculed and public service is denigrated, and I hope new candidates will keep it in mind when contemplating a run for public office. I also hope your book will help to inspire able men and women around the country to participate in public service."

❖ Recognize the fact that not everybody is going to vote for you.
❖ Don't take yourself too seriously.
❖ We become what we think about.
❖ As you sow, so shall you reap.

- ❖ I'm not perfect, you're not perfect, human beings are not perfect. We all have our faults, and we all have a lot to learn.
- ❖ The key word is Integrity.
- ❖ It's not what you have, it's what you do with what you have that counts.
- ❖ Force yourself to do public speaking. It gets a little easier each time.
- ❖ Either lead, follow, or get the heck out of the way.
- ❖ Don't be afraid you'll burn out. I'd rather burn out than rust out.
- ❖ Set goals. If you don't know where you're going, any road will get you there.
- ❖ A definite purpose is the starting point for all success.
- ❖ Jump in with both feet. Get involved. You are what you think you are.
- ❖ Practice, practice, practice.
- ❖ Believe in what you are doing.
- ❖ Be the best you can be. If you're not, you'll know it and be hounded by it the rest of your life.
- ❖ Get excited about life. Get excited about what you are doing.
- ❖ Occasionally laugh at yourself.
- ❖ Everything takes longer than you thought it would, costs more than you thought it would, and doesn't succeed as well as you thought it would.
- ❖ In politics, you have to tell 'em what you've done.

Wisdom, Thoughts, Truisms and Quotes

- In politics, all of Murphy's Laws are in effect.
- Every time you vote on something, you make half the people happy and half the people mad at you.
- Of the people you deal with, 99-1/2 percent are absolutely terrific, but the other 1/2 percent will drive you bananas.
- Things you plan are never as good as you think they should be, nor are they as bad as your critics would have you believe.
- Regardless of what you propose, you'll always find some people will have a problem with it.
- Be ready. When you get up at a public meeting and say something, the person after you is likely to get up and say, "Now, *that* is the dumbest idea I have ever heard." You need to develop tough skin.
- If you have a good attitude, you will survive anything.
- If you get something for "free," you really haven't gotten it free, you just haven't received the bill for it yet.
- If you are buying a house, beware of the real estate person who says that the beautiful lot across the street is where the city is going to put a park for the kids to play.
- In government, if someone proposes to paint the wall blue, it may end up with some blue in it. But it will also have some green, red, a yellow and orange as well, before it is finally approved by all those who have to pass judgment.

- ❖ People get turned off when a candidate becomes visibly angry. Stay cool, no matter what.
- ❖ Never say "Never," because never is a long, long time.
- ❖ Every minute of every day is not a Texas death match.
- ❖ In politics and life, it's "people dealing with people."
- ❖ Fifty percent of my advertising is wasted, but I don't know which 50 percent. *(George Washington Hill)*
- ❖ When the clock strikes 10, stop campaigning. You'll never get a vote after 10 o'clock at night.
- ❖ "The buck stops here." *(President Harry S Truman)*
- ❖ "People are always blaming their circumstances for what they are. I don't believe in circumstances. The people who get on in this world are the people who get up and look for the circumstances they want, and if they can't find them, make them." *(George Bernard Shaw)*
- ❖ "Four necessary attributes for success: Appetite, luck, the right people and fear. *(Sir James Goldsmith)*
- ❖ "Those who have never made a mistake work for those who dared to. *(Leon Sokolsky)*
- ❖ "You can't buy my vote, but it can be rented." *(Famous old-time politician)*
- ❖ Don't try to be politically correct. Just treat others with respect the same way you want to be treated. Do unto others as you would have them do unto you.
- ❖ "Politics has gotten so expensive that it takes a lot of money to even get beat with." *(Will Rogers)*

Wisdom, Thoughts, Truisms and Quotes

- Sometimes the people who make the rules don't play by the rules.
- "Every American mother seems to want their son to be President, but none wants him to be a politician." *(John F. Kennedy)*
- There are no original ideas in this world.
- If there is something in your past that can be dug up, it will be dug up.
- Some questions have more sides than a geodesic dome.
- To expand your rewards, expand your horizons.
- "Does he have a problem getting through the door considering his head is so big?" *(Paul Ingham)*
- So often the strongest, most persistent effort becomes the **winning** effort. Victory has a way of conferring her favor upon the one who tries the hardest.
- "Don't run too slick a campaign. People will think you're a politician." *(Nat Sorkin)*
- "Step aside and let a leader lead the way." *(Anonymous)*
- "Elections will be won by people who do their homework." *(Anonymous)*
- In politics, on one issue you and your fellow elected official may be 100 percent opposed. On the very next issue, you can be 100 percent in agreement.
- "When you play with the bull, you have to be ready to take the horns." *(A.D. Becker)*
- War is heck.

- "The game isn't over 'til the fat lady sings." *(A thousand people, especially at playoff time)*
- "Hey, Nick, you can't go 5 for 5 every night." *(Baseball great Vic Power)*
- "We're all on the same train going in the same direction. We're just not all necessarily eating out of the same bowl of nacho chips." *(Rich Becker)*
- "The state is what it is, because the people are what they are." *(Socrates)*
- Like selling Christmas trees, regardless of how good a salesman you are, there are certain times of the year they are tough to sell." *(Anonymous)*
- "We climbed the rough side of the mountain." *(Anonymous)*
- Have you noticed that the whole world is "at risk"?
- "Being a mayor is like being a bartender. They are always in your face." *(Anonymous)*
- There is a time for the speeches to stop and the action to begin." *(Anonymous)*
- You have to take the world as you find it.
- "The question is whether the government is going to control the individual, or the individual is going to control the government." *(Anonymous)*
- It's good to have a reputation for success.
- "This country was built by people, not by government." *(Anonymous)*
- Any jackass can kick down a barn, but it takes a carpenter to build one." *(Sam Rayburn)*

Wisdom, Thoughts, Truisms and Quotes

- "Quality is not an act, it is a habit." *(Aristotle)*
- "We all need to be responsive and responsible." *(Anonymous)*
- "You know the proposal was fair because everybody was mad about it." *(Larry Winn III)*
- "Campaigns are never hurt by confessions, only by discoveries." *(Anonymous)*
- "The shape of the future really doesn't have any physical shape. It must first exist in the mind." *(Anonymous)*
- "A rising tide rises all boats." *(Anonymous)*
- "We never talk about how we make sausage." *(Lee Atwater)*
- "You can't start a fire without a spark." *(Anonymous)*
- "You can make more friends in two months by becoming interested in other people than you can in two years by trying to get them interested in you." *(Dale Carnegie)*
- "I have discovered that many of us have no idea just how powerful we actually are. We are totally unaware of the tremendous reservoir of inner strength we possess." *(Wally Amos, after spending 50 years of research in the laboratory of life)*
- "Kids' sports activities are expensive, but you can spend it on softball fees now, or on bail bonds later." *(Bill Nicks)*
- "If you can't stand the heat, stay out of the kitchen." *(Harry S Truman)*

- ❖ It's the small things in life that are the big things.
- ❖ He was a very cautious man who never romped or played. He never smoked, he never drank, and he never kissed a maid. And when he up and passed away, his insurance was denied. For since he hadn't ever lived, they said he never died.
- ❖ "Don't let the facts get in the way of a good story." *(Bill Nicks)*
- ❖ "An electorate that is not heated by events is harder to stir than two-day-old oatmeal." *(George Will)*
- ❖ "Everybody is entitled to my opinion." *(Anonymous)*
- ❖ The reason I am so successful in business is that I buy an item for a dollar, I sell it for two dollars, and I'm happy with my one percent profit.
- ❖ The world is not an exact science.
- ❖ "It's what you learn after you think you know it all that counts." *(Harry S Truman)*
- ❖ "Elect me, because if I win, you win." *(Anonymous)*
- ❖ Life isn't always fair.
- ❖ You're judged on results, not on activity. The only thing that counts is what you've done.
- ❖ You are responsible for your actions.
- ❖ The three most important words you can say to yourself: "Yes, I can."
- ❖ "I will not be defeated by this or any other crisis." *(Rich Becker)*

Wisdom, Thoughts, Truisms and Quotes

- "Always check with your brother-in-law. He doesn't know anything about it either." *(Joe Dorsch)*
- "There are three ways for a politician to ruin his career: chasing women, gambling and trusting experts. The first is the most pleasant, the second the quickest, but trusting experts is the surest." *(George Pompidou)*
- "There is no free lunch." *(Anonymous)*
- "In this country we need more people pulling the wagon, and less people sitting in the wagon." *(Anonymous)*
- In a debate, when the age issue came up, Ronald Reagan said, "I will not exploit, for political purposes, the youth and inexperience of my opponent."
- "I don't care how great your ideas are or how well you can articulate them, people must **like** you before they will vote for you." *(Anonymous)*
- "I didn't do it all, but since I have to take the blame when things go wrong, I guess I can claim the credit when things go right." *(Anonymous)*
- "It's nice to be important, but it's more important to be nice." *(Anonymous)*
- Remember, those who participate make the decisions.
- "A journey of a thousand miles must begin with a single step." *(Laotse)*
- Get your thinking in order. "Nurture great thoughts for you will never go higher than your thoughts." *(Benjamin Disraeli)*

- ❖ "We should all be concerned about the future because we will have to spend the rest of our lives there." *(Charles F. Kettering)*

- ❖ "Nothing in the world can take the place of persistence. Talent will not; nothing is more common than unsuccessful men with talent. Genius will not; the world is full of educated derelicts. Persistence and determination alone are omnipotent. The slogan 'press on' has solved and will always solve the problems of the human race." *(Calvin Coolidge)*

- ❖ "Whatever your goals, you've got to bring your mental sensations into the picture. You've got to see your goals, feel them, taste them, believe them, enjoy them, ride in them…in your mind." *(Anonymous)*

- ❖ People have all kinds of ideas on how to succeed. Here's one that's true. "Unless you knock on that door, make that telephone call, write that letter, close that deal, do something, you won't see anything worthwhile happen in your life. Nobody is going to do it for you. You are responsible for your own success, so you've got to take the responsibility for making it happen." *(Anonymous)*

- ❖ "You are your own script writer, and the play is never finished, no matter what your age, position or place in life." *(Anonymous)*

- ❖ "Do not attempt to ingratiate yourself by offering favors; ask for them instead." *(Anonymous)*

- ❖ "Nobody's perfect. If I were perfect, I'd be Mayor of the city of Shawnee." *(Mayor Rich Becker, 1994)*

Wisdom, Thoughts, Truisms and Quotes

- This is not a perfect world.
- There is more than one side to *every* issue!
- More often than not, the little things make the difference between defeat and victory.
- "Act as though it were impossible to fail." *(Anonymous)*
- The only time to settle for what you have is when what you have is what you want.
- "Anyone who doesn't know what he wants will have to be satisfied with what he gets." *(George Bernard Shaw)*. And that seems to be the plight of most people.
- "One of the greatest stimulants for your imagination is an emotional involvement with your task. You've got to love whatever it is you are doing." *(Anonymous)*
- "I believe that if I give my best, and we do our best, we shall be the best." *(Ken Malach)*
- "Don't set wimpy goals. Set enormous goals." *(Robert Schuller)*
- "The best thing to do is to learn how other people get elected. In this way, the political novice will find out that there is no one rule that applies to everyone." *(James Roosevelt)*
- "Win, baby, just win!" *(Al Davis)*

Bibliography
Additional Sources of Information

National League of Cities
1301 Pennsylvania NW • Washington, DC 20004
(202) 626-3000

U.S. Conference of Mayors
1620 Eye Street NW • Washington, DC 20006
(202) 293-7330

National School Boards Association
1680 Duke Street • Alexandria, VA 22314
(703) 838-6722

National Association of Counties
440 First Street NW, 8th Floor • Washington, DC 20001
(202) 838-6226

National Conference of State Legislators
1560 Broadway #700 • Denver, CO 80202
(303) 830-2200

Republican National Committee
310 First Street SE • Washington, DC 20003

Democratic National Committee
430 S. Capitol Street SE • Washington, DC 20003
(202) 863-8000

Order Form

Please rush _____ copies of "Get Elected, Make a Difference!" by Rich Becker to:

Name _____

Address _____

City/State/Zip _____

Each book is priced at $22.00. Include $4.00 for shipping. Enclose check, or indicate credit card.

Bill my: ❏ Visa   ❏ MasterCard

Card No. _____ Exp. Date _____

Your Signature _____

Photocopy and mail this form with your check, or credit card information to:

Pump-Em-Up Publishing
9225 Woodstone Lane
Box 14934
Shawnee Mission, KS 66285

OR...Photocopy and fax this signed and completed form to:
913-894-9530

OR...Order by phone by calling:
1-800-711-7071

Order Form

Please rush _____ copies of "Get Elected, Make a Difference!" by Rich Becker to:

Name _____

Address _____

City/State/Zip _____

Each book is priced at $22.00. Include $4.00 for shipping. Enclose check, or indicate credit card.

Bill my: ☐ Visa ☐ MasterCard

Card No. _____ Exp. Date _____

Your Signature _____

Photocopy and mail this form with your check, or credit card information to:
**Pump-Em-Up Publishing
9225 Woodstone Lane
Box 14934
Shawnee Mission, KS 66285**

OR...Photocopy and fax this signed and completed form to:
913-894-9530

OR...Order by phone by calling:
1-800-711-7071